Knock 'Em Cold, Kid

Elaine Morgan

Matador
9 Priory Business Park,
Wistow Road, Kibworth Beauchamp,
Leicestershire. LE8 0RX
Tel: (+44) 116 279 2299
Fax: (+44) 116 279 2277
Email: books@troubador.co.uk
Web: www.troubador.co.uk/matador

ISBN 978 1780882 130

British Library Cataloguing in Publication Data.
A catalogue record for this book is available from the British Library.

Typeset in 12pt Bembo by Troubador Publishing Ltd, Leicester, UK
Printed and bound in the UK by TJ International, Padstow, Cornwall

Matador is an imprint of Troubador Publishing Ltd

This Book is dedicated to:

....⋆

⋆ *Please sign on the dotted line. In this day and age anyone who takes the trouble to write a book owes an increasing debt of gratitude to anyone who takes the trouble to read it.*

CHAPTER 1

Where I'm Coming From

I'd like to begin by introducing the four people with whom I spent the first nineteen years of my life. Let's begin chronologically with two grandparents, and meet them in the late 1890s

Fred and Martha

A steam engine pulls into Pontypridd station. Not many people get off because it's ten o'clock in the evening, a time when your average railway station would be pretty quiet. But Ponty station is never quiet for long because on one of the other tracks, another engine is pulling a long, long, long, long train of coal trucks clacketty-bang down towards Cardiff. That goes on night and day.

Among the passengers alighting is a young woman called Martha with a great mass of chestnut brown hair. She stands there with her young daughter and her even younger son worrying about whether she will be met. She needn't have worried. She is greeted and hungrily embraced by a man with an abundant yellow moustache, and a black line around his eyes like the mascara that Ramon Novarro and Charlie Chaplin will later wear in the silent movies. It's not mascara – it's coal dust, and at this date most of the men in Pontypridd have eyes like that, except that Fred's are blue. He's English, born in East Coker in Somerset, and so is Martha.

Their marriage broke up two years earlier because Martha, though of peasant stock like Fred, had acquired ideas above her station by working for some years as nursemaid to the squire's children, and Fred had turned out to be a scallywag poacher who gambled and drank. But after the split he'd come to South Wales to work in the pits and has recently written to her swearing that he's now a reformed character with gold sovereigns jingling in his pocket. He's put a deposit on a house in The Parade – that's the posh end of Pontypridd – and invited his estranged wife to come to Wakes with their two children, and live in it with him, and try to make a go of it. He picks up her luggage and leads her out of the station.

Unfortunately, it is Saturday night and chucking-out time. The coal rush in South Wales had some things in common with the Gold Rush in the Klondike, in that a horde of men of working age arrived there first, and it was the best part of a generation before enough women arrived to redress the balance and begin to civilise them. When Martha is led through Taff Street, it is crowded with drunken miners, singing or fighting and brawling, and some of this is conducted in an outlandish tongue. She has to shrink away from them and step over broken glass and men lying groaning on the pavement with blood pouring out of their noses. She is terrified and appalled. When they reach the Parade, the house is there as promised, but contains hardly any furniture. There are two beds, and once the children are in one and their parents in the other, Fred enthusiastically makes up for the last two lonely years and falls asleep with a smile on his face. Martha lies awake wondering in anguish what sort of place she has come to, and what sort of life awaits her.

Well, it was no bed of roses. She'd hoped to find some respectable friends, but it was not easy. The middle-class neighbours she would have liked to mix with took a dim view of hobnobbing with the wife of a man who worked underground, and her precarious pretensions to gentility did not endear her to the other women who might have made her welcome. Besides, she had, through no fault of her own, an English accent. To the natives that was known as a "twang", and talking with a twang indicated that you were showing off. She grew lonely and depressed, and since she was never one to suffer in silence, Fred soon grew as depressed as she was.

Things rapidly went from bad to worse. Fred was sacked from the pit. He'd been in charge of the pit ponies, and when a short-tempered miner got kicked by one of them and laid into the offending animal with his shovel, Fred attacked the man with his fists. Fighting underground is the sin against the Holy Ghost, so Fred's mining career was at an end. He found labouring jobs on the surface, navvying and road mending, and even an entrepreneurial venture to do with a fish and chip cart, but nothing prospered and their income was sporadic. As things got worse, Fred took to gambling again and Martha took to gin. They moved to a smaller house a little way up the Rhondda Valley, and got deeper into debt.

The dark day came when Martha lay in the grip of delirium tremens on what was assumed to be her deathbed, with the landlord vowing to evict the feckless widower and his offspring onto the streets immediately after the funeral. They sent for her sister, known as Auntie Jin, to come at once from Somerset if she wished to see Martha alive. She arrived, blamed it all on Fred, and observed that Martha had started to pluck at the sheets. In those days that was a sure sign that the end was very near, and since Martha showed no sign of recognising her anyway, she saw no point in hanging around. She went back to Yeovil.

That was the low point in the fortunes of Martha and Fred. The fact that they climbed out of it was entirely due to their daughter Olive, a winsome child with light brown ringlets, big blue eyes, bags of filial loyalty and considerable strength of character. At the age of ten she took charge of events. She nursed her mother throughout her self-inflicted illness, and cooked and cleaned and washed and mended and got her young brother Percy off to school. She pleaded with the landlord, swearing a Bible oath to bring him the rent each week plus a small sum off the arrears. On paydays she waylaid her father wherever he was working, and wheedled rent and housekeeping money out of his docket before the bookies could get hold of the rest.

Martha had been so terrified by the hideous creatures that had haunted her DTs that she promptly got herself "saved", by the very next Revival that swept through the valleys, and turned into a teetotal chapel-goer. But she never resumed her household duties. She found it much easier and more agreeable to leave all that to "our Oll", who had proved herself so capable. A message was sent to the school saying that Olive Neville's education must be considered at an end, as her mother was a permanent invalid and her services were indispensable at home. The teachers were indignant, because Olive's compositions had regularly been read out in front of the class, but there was nothing they could do.

Olive kept the household together and ruled it, not with a rod of iron, but by being hardworking, patient, sensible, and encouraging. They obeyed her orders – no, her suggestions – because they all knew that without her they'd be lost. In all my life I rarely saw her get angry and she seldom even raised her voice. One kind of behaviour did outrage her, and the story has come down to me of a moment in those early days when she went berserk. She saw through the bedroom window a baker's van man repeatedly kicking his horse in the belly as it stood between the shafts because it was too old and tired to go any further. Olive hurtled downstairs, grabbing a sweeping brush en route, rushed out into the road and began belabouring the man with the business end of it until it was wrenched out of her hand by a bystander. Like father like daughter, you see. But nobody was in a position to give Olive the sack.

You may be thinking that she sounds like a pastiche of the kind of young girls that Dickens writes about so sentimentally. She does indeed. But don't imagine those characters weren't based on fact. In Dickens's lifetime and for quite a stretch after he died, social conditions favoured the emergence of young females who had that kind of role dumped on them, and as often as not they rose to the challenge. (One of them even, improbably, strays into the alien world of P. G. Wodehouse's Lord Emsworth, lugging a young brother around with her and expressing a desire to pick some flahz.)

When she was fourteen, Olive was allowed to sit in on dress-making lessons being given to four sisters in the house across the lane, and their brother Billy would sometimes come into the room and gaze at her. Yes, you can see what's coming, can't you? You're dead right. Olive and Billy were my mother and father. So we must now put the Nevilles on hold for a while and cross over the lane and meet the Floyds.

Israel Floyd was an engineer of Cornish extraction who married a Welsh-speaking girl of farming stock, named Catherine Edwards. There was a family tradition that she was related to the William Edwards who in 1750 built Pontypridd's famous Old Bridge. An early studio photograph shows Israel and Catherine looking seriously bourgeois. Catherine is richly apparelled in bombazine, and Israel could easily have passed for Isambard Kingdom Brunel, if only Brunel had cultivated such an impressive moustache.

But Catherine's life, like Martha's, was soon on a downward slide, and became in the end so burdensome that she was glad to lay it down. When she was 76, she told my mother in confidence that she had resolved to carry on until she reached "my two sevens" and would then call it a day. And she did. She went to bed, turned her face to the wall (as they used to say), and quite quietly took her leave of the world in the space of five days. Sometimes when the campaign to legalise voluntary euthanasia is blocked for the umpteenth time by the House of Lords, the thought of Catherine is a comfort to me. Dying may be a thing that people (maybe animals too) have the capacity to decide to do, but most of us don't know it's there, so we're losing the knack of it.

What brought Catherine low was not only the economic blight that later settled over the whole area. There was also the fact that she bore fourteen children and followed the coffins of nine of them, at different ages, to the graveyard. One son was run over by a coal truck hurtling down the dram-road, had both his legs cut off and died before they could carry him home. When Catherine's own child-bearing days were over, she was presented with the newborn of her eldest daughter and brought him up too as her own. Olive thought the world of her, and the feeling was mutual.

Catherine was the archetypal Welsh Mam in all respects but one. The basic principle of Mamhood was that men and boys came first. That made sense in those days, certainly in a mining community. After all, they were the breadwinners. Their physical and psychological fitness had to be propped up at all costs, or everybody would be sunk. Catherine's five surviving children comprised four girls and the youngest child, Billy. In an ambitious family in that time and place, every spare penny would normally have been scraped together to get the boy educated and qualify him, if at all possible, for a job above ground.

Catherine thought otherwise. A boy, she reasoned, could always find work. (Those were the days). But what if one of her daughters failed to be wooed? Or at least wooed by anybody she could bear to marry? A fate worse than death might well await her. Not necessarily prostitution – but the phrase applied equally well in those days to such killing alternatives as taking in washing. Catherine therefore paid good money to have all her daughters taught dressmaking to a standard that would keep them respectably independent whatever happened.

So Billy left school at fourteen and got a job in the smithy as a blacksmith's striker. In his youth he was a very good-looking boy. Not tall – that was par for the area – but slim and lithe, with a dimple in his chin. Early photographs show him with a little-boy-lost expression, and soulful brown eyes. He could have passed for a poet. Beneath that deceptive exterior lurked the instincts of a practical joker – one of those pranksters who throw a comic light on human nature by selecting a victim and confusing the hell out of him. Billy loved making people laugh by any available means – telling funny stories, doing imitations, playing practical jokes, or concocting outrageous puns. In a different milieu he might have made a career as a stand-up comic. The other day I was reading about the early life of another Billy – Billy Connolly. A lot of it sounded strangely familiar. The difference was that Billy Floyd never had the luck to encounter anybody like Chick Murray, so he had no role model for taking to the boards. In the valleys in those days young men with a taste for histrionics who could hold an audience spellbound tended to end up in the pulpit.

I imagine practical joking was commoner then. It was a standard way of joshing the young, sending new apprentices to a shop to ask for a left-handed screw-driver or a tin of stripy paint. James Thurber describes some of these characters with a relish which makes me suspect that he too may have been a secret practitioner of the art. The boy Billy was a regular patron of a joke shop where you could buy imitation spiders and ink-blots and whoopee cushions, and cups that treacherously dribbled liquid down your front, and gadgets that made your plate move around the table, and buttonholes that squirted liquid, and jam pots that ejected a jack-in-the box when you unscrewed the lid.

Most people grow out of this, but Billy was very slow to kick the habit. I remember much later when I was about ten, a new couple with two young children moved in next door. The father was another joker and a hambo into the bargain, with a taste for amateur dramatics. He and Billy egged one another on. One Sunday Owen donned a wig and full drag. Billy solemnly walked up the length of Telelkebir Road with this flamboyant young tootsie clinging to his arm, tittupping along on her high heels, giving him flirtatious little slaps and tossing her curls brazenly at shocked onlookers on their way to chapel who stopped to stare. Billy walked into the house of his eldest sister Katie and introduced Owen as a cousin of Olive's on a visit from Somerset. Katie went into a flurry of embarrassment at the state of her house and apparel, wiping her hands on her apron and submitting to a surprisingly ardent cousinly kiss. Then the penny dropped. "Daft buggers the pair of you!!"

No-one was immune from these pranks except Olive. I remember once he called to me from his shed and when I put my hand on the latch to enter, I got an electric shock – a mild one, but enough to make me yelp. In Thurber's world such a childhood would reduce a character to a state of jumpy insecurity for the rest of his life. On me for some reason it had an opposite, immunising effect. I drew the conclusion that when life hurls things at you from unexpected quarters it's probably only joking, and these events are nearly always survivable as long as you don't take yourself too seriously.

But I've got ahead of my story. Back to Billy the kid. He fell in love with Olive Neville, as who wouldn't? At one time when she had an accident and wasn't allowed downstairs again for several weeks, he rigged up a pulley which ran from his bedroom window to hers, across the back lane which divided their houses, so that he could attach letters to it and send them bobbing across the line so that they couldn't be intercepted by her mother.

Soon they were going steady. Olive was just fourteen. They'd go for walks up the mountain side and find secluded dingles where they could lie in the grass and kiss. One day when they looked down at the little houses far below, Olive asked to borrow his telescope and he said he hadn't brought it with him. You have, I know you have, she said – I felt it just now, it's in your pocket. She wouldn't believe him until he'd held his arms out to be searched. It had to be one of his practical jokes but she didn't know why he was laughing or how he'd worked that trick. And if you're wondering how I know about it, I was told it over sixty years later, when under the influence of Alzheimer's the far-off days were more vivid in Olive's mind than the current ones, and she didn't know who I was. But by then she knew why Billy had laughed, and telling the story to somebody made her laugh too.

One week after the outbreak of World War One, Billy queued up to volunteer for France as a paid-up member of St. John's Ambulance brigade, and later enlisted in the Royal Field Artillery. Throughout the years in the army he carried a photograph of Olive in his pocket. It was pretty creased up by the time I got to see it. He wrote letters home to her, the first one beginning "Dear little English sweetheart". She kept that one, possibly because the tone was not typical of him and as the years went by he dropped the high romantic style and sent short letters or postcards, telling her briefly what was happening and trying to make her laugh. All the letters were signed simply "Yours, me." For the first few months he kept a diary, a vivid account of his impressions of leaving home for France and what it was like arriving there and seeing the first waves of the wounded coming into the wards.

After four years in combat, he'd acquired the skills that civvy street hadn't afforded him. He was a qualified fitter and rigger, so he would be able to support a wife when the war was over. He would not marry her before that date, urging that she should wait to see whether he came back alive and in one piece, with no limbs missing, in case she might have second thoughts about what she was letting herself in for. After the Armistice, he was asked to stay on for another year in the Army of Occupation in Germany to help with the rebuilding. He came home for a fortnight's leave to make plans for how they would marry as soon as he was home for good. He kissed her goodbye and went to join his unit. But there was a strike on, and the troopship couldn't leave port. The men were sent home again and told to report in another five days. Billy said "Oh what the hell!" and obtained a special licence and they were married at extremely short notice. Olive's only worry was that when he came home a year later he might, out of sheer force of habit, return first to his mother's house rather than his wife's. Luckily he passed the test.

However, snags had arisen. Billy, without much difficulty, found a job driving the fan in the Great Western Colliery, so they only had to find a place to live. There was a house for sale in Telelkebir Road, dilapidated and bug-ridden but repairable. However it was going to be hard to keep up the mortgage and at the same time do the necessary repairs to the structure and buy furniture. (Billy, though he didn't drink, was a chain-smoker and he couldn't face giving that up). Meanwhile, Martha was throwing a tizzy about how she could ever run her own household without Olive at her side. Olive was afraid that without close supervision her mother would grow depressed and return to her old habits.

She proposed a solution to both problems. Fred and Martha would for the time being move in with them, bringing their furniture and halving the burden of basic costs like the rates and the cost of heating. It was intended as a temporary solution to a temporary crisis. But it never ended. Billy died before ever having Olive to himself in a house of their own.

There were, predictably, tensions between Billy and Martha. She was short on humour and felt he didn't treat her with the respect she deserved. Religion was a sore topic because Billy held minority views on God. He could just about concede that some abstract being might have put the cosmic show on the road before losing interest in it, and he spoke no word against Olive continuing to attend her Baptist chapel. But nothing would induce him to set foot in the place himself, and Martha's new-found piety set his teeth on edge.

One evening she returned from a revivalist prayer-meeting, as hyped-up on salvation as she had formerly been on alcohol. Finding her husband, daughter and son-in-law sitting around the table peacefully enjoying a game of cribbage she swept all the cards into the fire, declaring in ringing tones that "Cards and dice are the devil's device!"

So that was roughly the set-up when I first put in an appearance in 1920.

CHAPTER 2

Childhood

Olive's baby was born at full term, sound in wind and limb, and named – though not christened – Elaine Neville Floyd. (Baptists don't christen babies.) Elaine wasn't a common name in the area, and it may have been suggested by Grandma Floyd. (The wife of her illustrious putative ancestor William Edwards had been called Elaine.)

However, the name wasn't used much in the house. My mother always called me Bunt, short for Bunting, from the lullaby "Bye, baby bunting, your daddy's gone a hunting." (It might seem that the anthropological image of Man the Mighty Hunter had been implanted in my mind at a very tender age, but that one was not a big game hunter. He'd only "gone to get a rabbit skin, to wrap the baby bunting in.")

My father's name for me was even more unpredictable. He was not given to sweet talk or sugary pet names. In those days a man referring to his wife would commonly call her his old woman. Billy started calling Olive "ol'ooman" on the way home from the wedding, and never after that called her anything else. Me he invariably addressed as "old hoss" – a bluff and matey term, but not a well-known local idiom. The miners' equivalent would have been "butty." Maybe he picked it up from officers on the Western Front, public school types who called each other things like old bean and old horse.

I was born, though not exactly with a silver spoon in my mouth, into a highly privileged environment. The privilege was the adult/baby ratio of four to one. It meant that during my waking hours I was very seldom left lying down sucking my thumb and staring at the ceiling. I could be passed seamlessly from lap to lap, being stimulated and talked to and coochy-cooched to my heart's content. Martha was always on hand to do this job. So was Gramp, between jobs and after work, while Billy, since he worked shifts at the colliery, was around in the daytime as often as not. Olive did the smallest amount of child-tending because she did everything else. It's hard these days to appreciate the hard slog of running such a household in the days before fridges, supermarkets, washing machines, vacuum cleaners, fast foods, electric or gas ovens, and central heating. Producing meals every day starting from ingredients like flour and raw potatoes was the first priority, but the task that Olive put her heart and soul into was the crusade against dirt.

The colliery was practically at the top of our street. Very little greenery survived in its vicinity. Where it did, you could pick a leaf and then find your fingers black with coal-dust. The children, like the miners, nearly all had blue scars – mostly on the knees, where they'd fallen down and the scabs had healed up over a lining of coal-dust. I've still got mine. It's faded almost to invisibility, but there are still a few grains of high-grade steam coal in there somewhere.

The house had an outside tap and no hot water. Every Monday Olive would repeatedly fill a heavy cast-iron boiler with water, balance it on the open fire to heat, and lug it out to two washing tubs in the back yard. Everybody's change of clothing and all the sheets, towels, etc. would be rubbed with a bar of soap and a scrubbing brush on a washboard, rinsed in a second tub of cold water, where appropriate blued and starched, put through an iron mangle, and hung up to dry. It took all day, and half of Tuesday went to ironing it.

The house itself was a battlefield against tracked-in dirt, the ubiquitous coal dust suspended in the air, the grime settling on the windows, smoke and ash from the open fire – and the pests. Olive had eliminated the bed bugs before moving in, but across the street was a public bakehouse where cockroaches (we called them blackpats) bred like flies and often sent out raiding parties across the road to colonise us. At great cost in time and toil, cleanliness reigned throughout the house and out as far as the white-stoned doorstep and the traditional semi-circle of scrubbed pavement for good measure. In her "spare" time

Olive did darning and mending and made clothes from paper patterns on the treadle sewing machine. So while she kept a close supervisory eye on my well-being, her role in my upbringing was not particularly hands-on.

For the first decade there was some anxiety. I didn't thrive. I was pasty-faced and plagued with frequent colds and coughs and sniffles and "bilious attacks" and caught every infection that was going around. Doctors looked at the white spots on my nails, said "anaemic", and prescribed horrible Parrish's food. They looked at me sideways and said "suspected curvature of the spine" but that was never confirmed. They looked at my stature – below average – and said "malnutrition". Olive was indignant – there was always good food in the house even though I couldn't keep it down – but they prescribed horrible Scott's Emulsion. (These things were not confined then to children of the proletariat. When I read Kingsley Amis's memoirs, I was moved to recognise the same white spots and the same Parrish's food.) I caught scarlet fever twice, which was supposed to be impossible – but perhaps the earlier spotty episode had been misdiagnosed. When I went to Grammar School I was the smallest but one of the year's intake.

However, I grew out of it. A great panacea in those days was the wholesale removal of tonsils and adenoids. Doctors prescribed it as a sensible precaution, a must, just as a generation later many of them promoted the circumcision of baby boys. Mass tonsillectomy sessions were held in the Pontypridd Cottage Hospital. I was taken there and anaesthetised, and awoke with a sore throat on the floor in a bare room with thirteen other children lying in two rows covered with blankets and showing no signs of life. It was like the anteroom to a battlefield. When I tottered out into the corridor I was told to go back and lie down again until everybody else woke up. But from then on – whether or not it was coincidence – I found myself gradually transmuting from a mewler and puker into a rather ungainly but sturdy and ravenous tomboy. Making up for lost time, I finally achieved a height of five foot two. That was just about acceptable, given the time, and the place, and the gender.

On account of ill-health in the early days, I was a bit late – five years old – starting school, but I was expected to do well there because I was already able to read. Gramp had taught me, without intending to, just by sitting me on his knee, reading aloud from an illustrated paperback book of nursery rhymes, and moving his finger along the lines as he read them out. This exercise proved so popular that it was endlessly repeated until the book virtually fell apart. I don't see how I could have avoided noticing that the J in the word that said Jack was the same shape as the J in the word that said Jill. And the same was true of the group of letters ending "Jill" and "hill." When Gramp first voiced his suspicion that I was reading, the idea was laughed off – but he turned out to be right.

On my first day at school I was startled to find that the local population outside number 54 failed to recognise my right to be the centre of the universe. Strange children to whom I'd never even been introduced felt entitled, for some reason, to criticise my behaviour and push me around. One incident on the first day seared itself into my memory. The class was given sheets of paper with shapes on and told to colour them in by moving the crayon in straight lines and in one direction only. Confronted with a triangle, I saw this was not the best way to proceed. I started filling in with strokes parallel to the three long lines, planning that these coloured areas would meet in the middle and nobody would be any the wiser. Hilda Clark put up her hand and grassed on me – "Miss, Elaine's doing it criss-cross" – and I was outraged by the stupidity of my elders and the gratuitous treachery of my peers. It took several weeks to cut me down to size, but it was all very salutary.

Apart from school, social life centred around the chapels. I attended Sunday school on Sundays, and the Band of Hope that met in the vestry on Monday evenings. The Band of Hope was dedicated to promoting total abstinence from alcoholic liquor. Its watchword, recited at every meeting, was "Touch not, taste not, handle not anything whereby thy brother or thy sister stumbleth." Females could also further the cause by use of the slogan: "Lips that touch wine shall never touch mine." One of my abiding memories is of the long benches we sat on, which had been inexpertly varnished, so that when you got up after sitting on them for any length of time, there was a kind of Velcro effect and a thin layer of fluff remained behind on the bench. We were shown lantern slides of things like diseased livers, and families reduced to penury, and what happened to a worm when you dropped it into a glass of whiskey.

It sounds absolutely dire, but the Band and the chapels also staged concerts where we could show off and do recitations – I did comic ones – and alfresco high jinks with egg-and-spoon races and lucky dips, and annual pantomimes. At one of these I was the wolf in Red Riding Hood. My mother made me a brown costume topped by a cardboard wolf's head with a movable jaw operated by a string. I turned in a spine-chilling performance, marred only by a scene-stealing child in the back row calling out: "Mam, that doggie's got shoes on!"

But the highlight of the chapel year was the outing to Barry Island. Each attendance at Sunday school was awarded with a ticket, and if you collected enough tickets throughout the year you were entitled to a free outing by train to the nearest seaside and a free sit-down meal in one of the restaurants on the waterfront. It was amazing, as the train chuffed south through the Vale of Glamorgan, to see the sky – a fairly narrow strip of the landscape in a place like Hopkinstown – widen and spread out until it was all around us. For most of us, that day in Barry Island was our only holiday. There was sea and sand, there were roundabouts and rock pools. It was absolute unalloyed Elysian bliss, dreamed of for months in advance – the months that move so much more slowly when you are a child.

The other longed-for annual event was Christmas. Naturally, the chapels made a big thing of it. There were special services with carol singing, and the sermons lightened up a bit. There were fewer stern warnings about the wrath of God, and fewer grisly details of Roman law-and-order methods (what Shaw called Crosstianity). Instead it was time to tell again the story of the little baby, the angels, the shepherds and the kings.

For high drama, come to number 54 in the early twenties. Now it came to pass that Pontypridd was rather low down on Santa's visiting list, so although he arranged for stockings to be duly filled by Christmas morning with a few nuts and chocolate coins in gold foil – and always a tangerine in the toe – he didn't put in a personal appearance until the evening of Christmas Day. It is six o'clock. The chicken dinner has been devoured. (Nobody I knew had turkey, but since we only had chicken once a year the effect was equally stupendous.) A fire has been lit in a room that at all other times is kept frigid and sacrosanct, ready to receive strangers on occasions like weddings, funerals, and visits by a clergyman or council official. The ceilings are draped from corner to corner with hand-made paper trimmings. There is a tree. The room is full of people because an aunt and uncle from Jenkin Street have joined us accompanied by their children. *There is a knock on the door!!*

Olive answers it and comes in to report that Santa has arrived but is suffering from a touch of snow blindness and would be grateful if the gaslight could be turned down a bit. He then enters with his sack. In the dimmed light his countenance is half-hidden by the hood and the whiskers, but his cheeks and even the backs of his hands look convincingly red and weather-beaten. His voice is strange – a little hoarse and breathy, but who can wonder after such a journey? In his sack there are presents for everyone, wrapped and labelled. Poor old soul, his attempts to read out the labels cause some nervously stifled amusement. My cousin Milwyn he addresses as "windmill" and he calls me "Ely Ales." The littlest cousin Valerie is so frightened by this apparition that she cowers behind the sofa.

There is of course a present for Billy, but Billy had been called out half an hour earlier by an alleged SOS from a family with a flooded kitchen in desperate need of a plumber. Santa seems displeased. He complains that the said Billy was absent last year too – allegedly putting in some sleep preparatory to a sixteen-hour shift. The suspense is terrible. I plead with the whiskered one to leave Billy's present (a stick of shaving soap) in my safe keeping, and he finally relents. After all it is Christmas.

But there was another side to Billy the clown, and it was perhaps the most powerful influence on my growing up. There was one good reason why Olive was able to preserve the peace in a household of not very well assorted characters living at uncomfortably close quarters. It was because Billy could always put space between himself and Martha by going out to his shed in the backyard. It was not very big, and it had a galvanised iron roof. But when, years later, I came across T. H. White's book *The Sword in the Stone,* and read how Merlin acted as tutor to the young Arthur, the set-up seemed strangely familiar. For me Billy's shed had been the equivalent of Merlin's cave.

It had everything in it, and only he knew where everything was. It was his kingdom and there he could afford to be serious. I was allowed in and learned the names of his treasures. His pride and joy was a massive screw-cutting lathe inherited from his father: the rest he had accumulated. A woodturning lathe, a brazier with bellows to make it glow white-hot. A cobbler's last with dubbin and heel-ball, a vice, bench hook, blowlamp, soldering iron, T-square, a great range of drills and fretsaws, screwdrivers, nuts and bolts, glass-cutters, rows of bottles of turps, and linseed oil for putty, and methylated spirits, tins of paint and creosote, spanners and pliers and pincers and hacksaws and rasps, sheets of emery paper, magnets, crystals, and an eye-glass for mending watches, and a hundred other things I have forgotten.

He could mend anything for anybody. He bitterly regretted that he "couldn't do the logarithms" – in the army he had met an officer with a little book that would magically supply him with answers to problems – but Billy could always find a way around that by "trial and error". He was fascinated by technology and science, even the bits he didn't understand. He could talk to me unguardedly because there was no danger that I'd laugh at him, and there were things he thought I should know. I remember when he found out and told me – years before the school told me – that the air is kept in balance because we breathe in oxygen and breathe out carbon dioxide while plants appear to do the opposite. He thought long and hard about the quest for a perpetual motion machine and wondered whether someone – (who?!) – might one day hit upon the way to achieve it.

He taught me to be sceptical and not to be afraid. There are no such things as ghosts. There is no such place as hell. There is nothing in the dark that wasn't there before the candle was blown out. Perhaps he had hoped for a son but I was the next best thing and he expected me to be brave. Once in Ynysangharad Park when quite young I got transfixed with terror at the top of the long slide and made a nuisance of myself pushing past everybody on the ladder to get back to ground level the safe way. Billy was on a bench nearby. He gazed into the distance and never said a word but I had seen his expression. I climbed the ladder again and went down the slide. Nothing to it really. Like the ghosts.

Here are some examples of the kind of things we did in the shed. I remember the iron filings on a pane of glass that waved like grass in the wind when the magnet moved beneath them. I remember pouring drops of molten tin foil from a height into a bucket of cold water, and admiring the strangely sculptured artefacts that could be fished out of the water afterwards. I learned to clean mercury by squeezing it through a square of muslin – it descended in a shower of silver rain and the dirt stayed behind on the rag. I learned that if you put a stick of filed aluminium into a test tube of mercury it will, in the course of a few days, grow a white beard made of some kind of crystals.

And here's a biological experiment. Upend a large hammer in a tin bath of water so that the end of the handle makes a little island, and place a spider on the island to see what it will do. When we did it, I knelt beside the bath to watch and after a while it rose on some of its back legs and began to wave the front ones and do a little dance. I couldn't see the fine line of silk it was floating out into the void in the hope that it would catch onto something. I only saw it climbing up through thin air towards a spot between my eyebrows. I couldn't move before it landed because this was an "experiment", and science was sacred. I've told the story more than once and a few people have repeated the experiment with different results. The strategy deployed seems to vary according to the species of spider.

If anyone ever writes a paper on it, I hope they'll give a footnote to Billy.

CHAPTER 3

Hard Times

I have no memory of feeling deprived as we entered the Hungry Thirties. Billy, like millions of others, lost his job in 1929. But I don't remember having any clear sense that times had once been better. Everyone around us seemed to be in more or less the same boat, and none of us had television sets advertising all sorts of wonderful consumer goods that we couldn't afford. In that kind of situation life is pleasanter for children than for the grown-ups who have to do the worrying.

For one thing I certainly never went hungry. It's true that there were some children in my class at primary school who were often hungry, and if you went down the street eating an apple they would follow you and say "Can I have the stump?" In winter some of them came to school in thin dresses or not at all. They looked tired and vacant-eyed and one or two caught TB and died. I was never in any doubt about how lucky I was.

First, I'll try to explain the finances of it. In our family we started off with two built-in advantages. There were two doles coming into one house and that was in itself an economic plus. There was one child instead of three, or seven, or ten. That was uncommon, and made all the difference in the world. Olive wanted at least one more child (preferably a boy) but Billy wouldn't have it – it was one of the very few respects in which she didn't get her own way in her own house. On top of that there were three other considerable advantages. They were Olive's competence – which has already been indicated – and Gramp's allotment, and Billy's odd jobs.

Olive had for years been saving money in a special box designed to fulfil one day the dream of her life: to have one of the bedrooms converted into a bathroom. Billy could do all the work if she could save enough for the materials. After 1929 she stopped putting money into it, and after a few years on the dole the box was empty.

Gramp had his name down for one of the allotments a mile or two away in Coedpenmaen, and his name came up at just the right time. There wasn't much of a waiting list, because miners in general tended not to be passionate gardeners. There were no gardens in their houses for them to cut their teeth on, and after a hard shift underground there was no inclination to seek out any form of healthful exercise. The real stroke of luck was that the owner of the adjoining allotment was getting too old to cope with it and instead of handing it back to the council he let Gramp take it over, for a small consideration in the way of free produce.

Gramp had been born and bred on the land and now had room to spread himself, and he was very good at it. So we had free fresh vegetables nearly all the year round, and fruit in season. He grew potatoes, carrots, parsnips, swedes, cabbages, Brussels sprouts, (no leeks, I don't know why) and kidney beans and broad beans, and raspberries and gooseberries and strawberries. Just one drill he reserved for non-utilitarian purposes. He cherished every year a crop of sweet peas climbing up on sticks like the runner beans. They had a long flowering season and strong straight stems and came in most of the colours of the rainbow, and they smelled like heaven.

At home Gramp was almost totally taciturn, but once every year he came into his own, produced a sheet of paper, and initiated and chaired a discussion, chiefly about potatoes. We, the consumers, were asked which kinds we wanted him to plant and in what quantities. Did we want first earlies or second earlies? Floury ones recommended for mash and for chips, or nice firm waxy ones to provide lovely little new potatoes for boiling? How many King Edwards? How many Arran Banner?...There were times when he got a bumper crop of something. He might trundle a wheelbarrow back to the house containing a sackful of runner beans and flog them off up and down the street at half the price the shops were charging. But Olive proposed that what he collected on these rare occasions was his perk, and well earned, even if he did go straight out and put it on a horse. And nobody demurred.

Billy in those years became a sort of factotum to most of Hopkinstown. He could do anything – put new glass in your window, new slates on your roof, new leather soles on your shoes, new brakes on your bike, a new leg for your table that perfectly matched the other three, mend clocks and watches, or put in a new pipe if your plumbing sprang a leak. The place at that time was running alive with children and they were some of his most faithful clients, asking him to deal with scooters whose wheels had come off and dolls whose arms had come off. He had a little box full of nothing but dolls' eyes, the kind that open and shut and don't survive rough treatment. They were salvaged from patients whose smash-ups had proved beyond repair, and used for transplants into new casualties.

Those neighbours who were out of work (the majority) were charged nothing for labour. For resoling shoes, for instance, he accepted no more than the cost of the leather, because he was not short of time, and was always happier doing something than doing nothing. The formula was: "Ta, Billy, what do I owe you?" "Oh, just hang it on the hook." That phrase puzzled me and puzzled some of his clients, but in practice it meant that there was nothing to pay. Sometimes somebody would come to the back door at a future date with a fish caught in the reservoir, or a rabbit killed with a catapult. If not it didn't matter, and didn't stop them coming again when the need arose. The formula for the slightly more solvent was "Call it a packet of fags." A packet of fags was a small open-ended container – paper, not cardboard – containing five Woodbines, and it cost two pence.

One of the more bizarre requests I remember was from an old man suffering great pain from one of his few remaining teeth. He couldn't afford to go to a dentist and in those days the NHS wasn't even a gleam in Nye Bevan's eye. He was in too much distress to bother about a detail like the lack of an anaesthetic. Billy examined the problem, found the tooth seemed to be a bit loose already, washed his hands. and selected a suitably sized tool from among his pincers and pliers. The operation was a success. Another satisfied customer.

But — and here we come back to proper market economics — he could also keep an internal combustion engine in proper working order, even if it was well on in years, and sometimes even if it was a model for which spare parts were no longer available. He could examine a broken constituent part and make an exact replica. It goes without saying that no private individual in Hopkinstown had a motor car, except the family in the big house at Hafod Fawr. But some of the tradesmen by then had vans instead of horses and carts, and a pressing need to keep them on the road. And he didn't need Olive to remind him — as she would have been swift to do — that in these cases it would have been madness to say "Hang it on the hook."

So neither Fred nor Billy was idle. There were only three snags. (1) Most of Billy's customers were skint (2) demand from the paying customers was sporadic and might turn up only seven or eight times in a year and (3) he was operating on the fringe of the law, and the streets were policed by an army of Means Test Men, who paid unheralded visits from time to time to check up on dole claimants.

Gramp was immune to these worries. They couldn't dock your dole on the grounds that you put seeds into the ground and ate what grew out of them. But it was illegal for Billy to perform any task for financial reward without informing the authorities. Strictly speaking he should have kept records reading: "Soldered Jack Jones's kettle: two pence. New pulley in Mrs. Pugh's clothes line: thruppence." In theory these amounts could be deducted from the money they gave him. But they wouldn't really have wanted all that paperwork.

So many of the jobs that were carried out in the shed went unreported — they were part of the black economy. I'm not arguing the morality of it. Sometimes, if he was working in the open, he did sign off, because with all due respect to working-class solidarity, there were one or two people around who would grass on you. One day there were gale force winds that left a number of houses in one street with slates off. By working fast, Billy was able to repair them all within seven days, earning more than enough to compensate for foregoing a week's dole. I remember this because the Means Test Man called, perhaps more in sorrow than in anger, saying it had been rumoured that Billy had been seen working. Was this true? Billy said yes. And had he remembered to sign off the dole? Yes of course, said Billy piously, and the Means Test Man was left speechless. Such quixotic behaviour was so rare that he hadn't even bothered to check.

So that was the general set-up, none of it of much concern to the old hoss, who was busy growing up. I created a bit of a stir at the age of eleven. I'd written a little story for my own amusement, and the exercise book on my desk was found during playtime by the teacher and passed on to the governess, who asked to borrow it and secretly posted a copy to "Wales's National Newspaper", the Western Mail. They printed it in the weekly magazine supplement called the Weekly Mail, and came and photographed me and paid me a guinea. Some people were impressed, but others said it was a great con and Billy must have written it.

For British children in 1931, the eleven plus was, in social terms, the great divide. All the friends I knew from primary school went on to Mill Street Secondary, and I went on to the girls' grammar school and entered an entirely new world. There were I think only four from the Rhondda ward in form 2a, and we sat one behind the other at the window side of the room. Pontypridd was the commercial hub of the valleys and most of the other pupils came from its more prosperous sectors.

They had better manners and much better accents. When it was time to pay dinner money on Fridays they went up to the desk and handed in money while the Rhondda lot sat tight, because dinners for children of the unemployed came free. The English mistress Miss Faraday had grey hair and beautiful enunciation, and when she asked pupils to read poems aloud, you could see her close her eyes and wince at what some of us did to the English tongue. It's hard to believe now how widely the vowels differed even within that room. For a word like "pure" some of us said "pewer" while Miss Faraday wanted to hear "pyaw". All the same I was mesmerised by the lessons, gulping in great draughts of culture, while Iris in the seat behind prodded me and whispered her own reaction to Miss Faraday: "Haven't she got low down titties?"

You will now be subjected to a pet anecdote illustrating what a show-off I was in those days (and must be still, or I wouldn't be repeating it). Miss Faraday went round this new class of eleven-year-olds asking each of us what we wanted to be when we grew up. Not a single one said: "I hope to marry and bring up children." Instinct told us that that was not on the menu, even though in the real world it was the likeliest outcome. They said they wanted to be nurses or librarians, teach infants, or work in some (unspecified) shop or office. Iris behind me said she hoped to be a ladies' hairdresser. I said "I'm going to be an etymologist."

Miss Faraday was silent for a second or two. "Do you know what it means?" "Yes. It's about the history of words." No comment. But I thought "At least you now know I'm not pyawly thick." I had by then joined the public library, and was acquiring words like that at the rate of one or two a week, many of them from Kipling. He was easy to read, but he refused to dumb down his vocabulary, and I could look up the long words in the dictionary – one of the four books we had in the house. (The others were Wuthering Heights, Arthur Mee's Children's Encyclopaedia, and a comically illustrated "Ruthless Rhymes for Heartless Homes" – a parting gift to Martha from the squire's wife.)

I soon made friends. I remember two in particular, widely contrasted. Priscilla was from my own social stratum, and her arrival in grammar school was far more of a miracle than mine. She was one of eight children, and her mother kept the family solvent by opening a sweet shop. Priscilla had bags of vitality and imagination so we laughed a lot, and sometimes got so deep in conversation that we walked back from Treforest to Pontypridd along the canal bank instead of catching the bus.

Peggy was at the opposite end of the social spectrum. Her father had been a notable and controversial figure in Pontypridd public life, and she'd attended a small local private school instead of the local elementary. When she was nine years old, her mother interrupted the story she was telling to go out to the kitchen, where she dropped dead. Her husband died not long afterwards. Since the orphaned Peggy was the youngest of five siblings, they proceeded to bring her up in accordance with their own liberal principles. One sister was a doctor, another took over the chore of running the house, a brother was a medical student. All that may help to explain why she was – like many of the liveliest heroines in the "Schoolgirl's Own" magazine – "the naughtiest girl in the school."

She quite sincerely felt herself to be in all respects the equal of the teachers. She would argue with them over details like the latest estimates of the true height of Mount Everest – and would sometimes be right. She once walked all across the narrow ledge of the balcony in the Assembly Hall just to see if she could do it; if she had fallen she would certainly have been hospitalised. One teacher said in exasperation: "If you think you can take this class better than I can, you'd better come out here and do it!" Mistake. Peggy found it a quite reasonable suggestion. She went to the front and said: "Now class, I want you to open your textbooks and turn to page 23." Most impressively of all, when a group of girls were giggling in the cloakroom over some rumour – picked up in the gutter no doubt – about boys and babies, Peggy corrected them. She gave a brief and concise account of the generative process in *Homo sapiens*, with no giggles at all. We were stunned.

I had no dealings with Peggy outside school, and at the age of sixteen the family moved to London, where she later had to be dug out of the rubble after the blitz, not much the worse for wear. But while she was in Pontypridd I was deeply impressed by her anarchist attitudes to authority and her conviction that all things were possible. She was a remarkable girl and in course of time produced an equally remarkable daughter – the publisher Victoria Barnsley.

But now, since sex has (in the long-forgotten cliché) reared its ugly head, comes the question: "What about boyfriends?" The answer is zilch. There were no boys I even got to talk to. At around seven or eight I'd tried to hang around and join in when they played games like cricket in TVR lane, because they seemed on the whole to be doing more interesting things than girls were doing. I offered to be a fielder. No dice, needless to say. A couple of years later Olive developed an obsessive anxiety to keep me away from the opposite sex. Once, informed that I'd been seen sitting on a windowsill with two other girls talking to boys, she came and detached me, and I was ignominiously led back home. In hindsight I can see the motivation. She wanted a great life for me and knew all those hopes would go down the drain if I ever fell from grace and became pregnant. At the time I deeply resented it, feeling it could have been more diplomatically done. But of course it was the lack of diplomacy that made it effective: the humiliation of it ensured that I wouldn't readily risk a repetition.

It gradually became borne in on me that she needn't have worried. I began to fear there was something wrong with me. Some girls of my age were beginning to attract the focussed attention of boys but for some reason I was to all intents and purposes invisible to them. Their eyes passed over me with no more flicker of interest than if I'd been a housewife of forty-two. I'd had all those years of being the old hoss, the tomboy, delivering comic rhymes like "My face I don't mind it, 'cos I am behind it", and among my prettier cousins being introduced, with a touch of apology, as "And this is Billy's daughter Elaine. She's the brainy one." (Ouch.)

Throughout the free and lovely sexless years of roaming the hills and climbing trees and admiring beetles and bluebells and birds' nests, it had never bothered me for an instant. I've been assured by older people who remember me from that time that I was okay: there was nothing wrong with the way I looked. But there was a hell of a lot wrong with my self-image. I began to grow bulges on my chest, somewhat sooner than expected, but if you think that helped you couldn't be more wrong. I hated them, and not only because they looked damn silly under a gymslip. They were also (you have to be pretty old not to find this incredible) unfashionable. We were at the tail end of the flapper era, when the Bright Young Things aspired to a boyish silhouette, and top models strapped their breasts down to keep them flat, as ruthlessly as their Victorian predecessors had cinched in their waists. I had grown up believing that having breasts was unforgivably dowdy.

Michael Frayn nailed my state of mind accurately when he described one of his characters anguishing over the fact that she wasn't a girl, not in any real sense of the word. "She was just a young female human being, fit only to be somebody's cousin or aunt." I was one of those, and became increasingly anxious about it.

On the home front there came a major and disastrous development. It was the result of a turn of the screw by the government in response to the huge burden of the very high rate of unemployment, and it was made worse in our case by unlucky circumstance. The existing Household Means Test was replaced by the more stringent Family Means Test. You might be out of work through no fault of your own, but if you had kith and kin still in employment, even if they lived far away, they were obliged to contribute to your upkeep. Gram and Gramp had such a relative. Their son Percy, Olive's younger brother, was a baker's van man, married with two children. The Means Test Man dropped in to advise them that Percy could reasonably be expected to pay five shillings a week and their income would therefore be reduced by that amount.

The snag was that with the best will in the world Percy couldn't do it. A few miles away he had another family to support – another woman, and two other children. This was a very shameful thing and was supposed to be a dead secret. It was of course known in our house. Even I had a rough idea that something was up, because Uncle Percy often dropped in, and couldn't restrain himself from proudly passing around pictures of a new baby he had just happened to meet and photograph while on his bread round. It seemed out of character somehow.

The Means Test Man's declaration flummoxed Gramp. He cleared his throat. "The thing is – " he began – but he got no further. Martha got to her feet, drew herself up to her full height, and took up a position between him and the Means Test Man. She was convinced that Gramp was about to publish the family scandal to the world. Everyone would get to hear about it, and that would bring her white hairs in sorrow to the grave. It was not to be borne. Percy was in any case the apple of her eye, much dearer to her than Olive who did everything for her.

She put on her grandest air, based on the demeanour of her role model the squire's wife, and said smoothly that naturally she would only have to mention it and her devoted son would be only too proud and pleased to be able to help in this way. The relieved inquisitor was not accustomed to getting such an easy ride, but he thankfully made a note to that effect and left. We all knew that from then on the family would be "deemed" to be receiving money that was not there. Five shillings may not seem much, but the dole in those days was twenty-six shillings a week. Olive was shaken, but loyally remained silent.

At the time it was a considerable shock. Billy abruptly got up and left the room and went out to fume in the shed. He must have been incensed by what Martha had done – and also, as he often was, by her way of doing it. Two things kept him from exploding. One was that he couldn't rant and rave without further distressing Olive who was, God knows, distressed enough already. But there was also the possibility that if he openly tangled with Martha, he might get as good as he gave. He was not without his Achilles' heel.

In fact he had two of them. For one thing he was still addicted to his Woodbines. Often he would have one behind his ear, ready to light from the one in his mouth before putting it out. It saved matches. For another thing there was a slight impression abroad, sometimes mentioned to Olive by the neighbours, that it was hard to understand why a man of such talents had not found himself a regular job. True, nothing was on offer from the Labour Exchange, but some people rightly observed that he didn't "push himself." He might have somehow got hold of a decent suit, and donned the collar and tie that was reserved for funerals and always looked as if it was strangling him, and persuaded people to write references to his abilities, and turned up uninvited on the doorsteps of the people in the seats of power, knocking on doors, either cringing or masterfully eloquent, banging on desks, demanding or pleading "Gissa job." He did none of those things.

Olive didn't (to my knowledge at least) make an issue of it because she knew the man she was married to, and he was constitutionally incapable of pushing himself. I don't know whether this is a particularly Welsh characteristic: sometimes I think it is.

That change in the Means Test rules was disastrous. Up to then, though her life involved hard work, Olive seemed, and I believe was, happy with her lot. Compared to the situation and prospects that had faced her at the age of ten, she had come through with flying colours. She had health and strength, a house and a husband and child, she was loved and obeyed by everyone in the family, admired for her creative talents in the realms of cookery and needlework, and had the respect and approval of her neighbours. Money isn't everything.

But hope deferred maketh the heart sick, and at that point things seemed to be getting worse, not better. I wasn't much aware of it. Adolescents can get pretty self-absorbed in negotiating the rocky road between being a child and assuming the guise of an adult, and there were things going on in my head that she didn't know about either. But when I did get glimpses of what it was like for her I felt ashamed of being so obtuse. Two examples come to mind.

It got harder and harder to replace things that wore out. When sheets got thin, you could get a few months' more wear out of them by slitting them up the middle and joining the outer edges together, but you couldn't do that with clothes. You had to handle them with extra care so that the thin bit wouldn't actually become a hole. One day when Olive was ironing one of her wrap-around aprons, despite her care the point of the iron went right through it. She threw it on the floor and danced on it in a kind of revenge, because she'd got sick of it and now would never have to wear it again. Since I wasn't a girly girl and the whole thing about clothes bored me stiff, it had never got home to me that she'd been a beautiful girl and was a good-looking woman and never got a chance to dress for the part. And she minded.

Years later during the war I was given a clue to what it had really been like for her. I'd taken a vacation job in London and asked her to come up for a few days and took her to places like St. Paul's Cathedral and a theatre matinee. The play by Dodie Smith was, like most plays at the time, a saga of middle-class life, but among the minor characters was a man who'd lost his job. In one scene, he and wife put their arms round one another and wept. To my surprise Olive's cheeks were wet too, and she told me that she and Billy had done that sometimes. She wondered aloud how the playwright could have known a thing like that. How indeed? I lived with them and I'd never guessed it.

There were expenses involved when I passed the eleven plus. There was, for example, a school uniform to be obtained from a special rather expensive outfitter's. Olive swallowed her dislike of anything looking like charity and applied to the British Legion, which had a small fund to help ex-servicemen's families down on their luck. They gave me a blazer – not the standard one but a cheaper equivalent: you could sew a badge on it and nobody was supposed to notice. They also gave me a thick warm winter coat. It was not supposed to fit, because it had to last several years and you were meant to grow into it.

Billy put metal studs on the bottom of my shoes to prevent them from wearing out so quickly, and whenever I broke into a run, one shoe would kick the opposite ankle and the metal studs would make it bleed. I was fascinated when I discovered from the dictionary that some horses – presumably those with a gait as awkward as mine – do exactly the same thing, and there is a special word for the resulting lesions. I've always wanted to use this word so here goes: in my adolescence, like many another old hoss, I suffered from crepances.

One thing happened to make the tough times a little bit easier financially. Billy couldn't push himself, but there was one other difficult thing he could do and he did it. He gave up smoking, and did it cold turkey, with no patches or anything else to help him. It was one period in his life that was no joke. For weeks we all treated him as somebody fragile, not to be approached without special unction and consideration, metaphorically on tiptoe. In a strategic move that was typical of Olive's attitude to life and people, the money that was not being spent on Woodbines did not immediately go into keeping the family afloat. Every penny of it went into one of those little boxes. This one was the Vice Box – not because smoking was a vice, but because it was earmarked for the purchase of a really strong gripping tool that Billy had once seen in John Hall's and coveted ever since. When the required sum had been saved, the two of them went together on the train to Cardiff and bought the vice and brought it home. By then the worst of the withdrawal symptoms were over. Billy never smoked again, and the gap in their income created by Percy and the Family Means Test had been narrowed.

So in one way and another, we weathered the worst time. *Nil desperandum*. Or, in the version that Billy brought home from the Western Front: "Nil carborundum" – never let the bastards grind you down.

CHAPTER 4

Schooldays

Everyone said I took after Billy. That wasn't an unmixed blessing. I often wished I had inherited Olive's abundant wavy hair, striking blue eyes, and trim waist. But as far as temperament goes, the paternal genes would appear to have been dominant, and I do regard that as a stroke of luck. It was undoubtedly Olive's temperament that kept the show on the road, and without her I would have got nowhere. But it was less of a blessing for her. Among other things it meant that she did all the worrying for both of them – for all of us – while Billy had the knack of totally ignoring "unborn tomorrow and dead yesterday". He was content to get the very best out of the day he was living through, in the confidence that it would all come right in the end. And there's a fair amount of that in me. I'm aware that such people can sometimes be a bit exasperating to live with, but on the other hand two worriers in the same partnership wouldn't be a very good recipe either.

In the grammar school, once I found my feet, I was a square peg in a square hole. There was a lot they wanted to teach me, and not much limit to what I wanted to know. I didn't shine at everything. In sports I was a dead loss. We played tennis in the summer and I was lucky if I won one game in ten. We played netball in the winter and I have memories of shivering miserably in some corner of the field hoping the ball wouldn't come my way. My fingers used to go white up to the knuckles, and really hurt when we got in out of the wind and the blood forced its way back into them.

At art I was just about adequate. Our art mistress was called Miss Prinsep. Years later, when researching the life of Stanley Spencer, I discovered that a man called Prinsep had been a leading light in the Slade School of Art, so I imagine that's where she came from. She was good at her job. Most of them were. In those days teaching in a girls' grammar school was one of the more desirable options for intelligent young women of any class as long as they were content to remain single. (Marriage entailed instant dismissal.)

Throughout the years of tuition, Miss Prinsep only once gave me a word of personal commendation. We'd been told to paint a wall. The temptation is to draw a wall – any fool can do that, you just put black lines around all the bricks – and then colour it in. But I'd noticed that the mortar in this wall was lighter than the bricks, and painted it that way. "Mmm... yes, you really looked at it, didn't you?" she murmured. I was so bucked I tried really looking at a lot of other things. I suppose that's one of the points of teaching art.

The music mistress was Miss Hughes. She taught us to sing in harmony, but something was going wrong with the harmony. She asked us each in turn to come out to the front and sing a scale, and thus tracked down the source of the problem, which was Elaine Floyd. She asked me quite nicely to keep my mouth shut from then on, or if I wanted to open it to show willing, to make sure that no sound came out of it. Miss Hughes's music lessons were successful because on the whole the girls enjoyed singing, but when she took us in other subjects her lessons were something of a shambles. She couldn't keep discipline and I'm afraid we exploited that and "took advantage" of her. She wasn't really cut out for teaching and maybe had entered the profession because she had a livid birthmark on one side of her face, and hoped that in an all-female establishment it would matter less.

During one vacation she paid to have an operation to remove it. She turned up on the first day of term with a large dressing still in place, and in her eyes a mixture of apprehension and defiance. She needn't have worried. The girls reacted rather as the electorate reacted to Mo Mowlam when she appeared in public with a shorn head after a brain tumour operation. They became protective, obliging, and obedient. A year later, when it was announced at the end of term that

Miss Hughes was leaving to get married, she was cheered until the rafters rang.

Then there was Drama. In primary school we'd only had one visiting teacher who encouraged us to act. Ambitiously, she selected short scenes from Shakespeare. I was Bottom (wouldn't you know). I chiefly remember this because Billy heard me rehearsing "I gleek upon occasion", and used to tease me by asking how I was getting on with my gleeking. But in the grammar school, drama was quite a big deal. There was an annual School Play, to which parents were invited. After four years in the lower forms as a mere spectator, I graduated to the point of being auditioned for small parts like The Messenger or The Maid. You couldn't have someone playing the lead in a serious drama with an accent like Max Boyce. (The perceptive reader might observe that that plea is a cop-out. Quite possibly I only got small parts because I couldn't act any better than I could sing. It's a fair comment.)

I didn't care though. It was thrilling just to be part of it, and watch Maidie Cohen acting her socks off and keeping everyone enthralled. I'd read a lot of plays from Pontypridd Library, including the whole of Shaw. I knew what things like "Exeunt" meant even though I pronounced it to rhyme with "fluent." Everything about play-acting flashed up in my mind if not in lights, at least in capital letters. I was there, I was a part of it. We had Props and a Producer. I was Back Stage, in the Wings, waiting for my Cue. And I was there at the end of the row when we took the Curtain Call.

Term-time wasn't the whole story either. The school fostered a branch of Urdd Gobaith Cymru, the Welsh League of Youth. They ran summer camps, which I attended for three consecutive years. Some weeks were reserved for native Welsh speakers and others for dysgwyr (learners). They were segregated by sex too. I don't know whether the boys' camps were in different weeks or in a different place.

Our camp pitched its tents in Llangrannog, a beautiful and remote spot on the west coast – the equivalent of the Irish Gaeltacht, where among the local population Welsh was the standard means of communication for young and old. It was the first time I'd slept away from home, and I found the nights incredibly quiet without the noise of the trucks at night. The camp was run mainly by young women not very much older than we were. Some were students at Aberystwyth University. They were passionately devoted to the ideal of preserving the language, and the counter-culture that went with it, to provide a corrective to the Empire Day/Union Jack ethos that pervaded the text-books of the school's history curriculum.

There were some organised activities but it was not too regimented, and sometimes I wandered off on my own to explore the little coves, and cross to Lochtyn Island at low tide. Once I was enraptured to find half a dozen seals floating upright in the water quite close to the rocks I was sitting on. I sang to them. They didn't sing back but they stayed quite a long time, all gazing at me, apparently with the same absorbed curiosity that kept my eyes riveted on them. It was magic.

The other snapshot in my memory is of the evenings, coming out of the big hut after a *cymanfa ganu* (singing session) and heading down over the grass towards the tents. Lamps had been lit inside them to light us to bed, so that they glowed at the bottom of the field like rows of Chinese lanterns, and behind them the moon was rising over the Irish Sea.

So, barring small glitches and occasional spasms of foreboding about my lack of sex appeal, life flowed along like a song. In the academic subjects I came top with monotonous regularity and got nine O-levels, and the school began to consider entering me for Oxford. That was an ambitious project, because no girl had ever gone on to Oxford from the Pontypridd Intermediate School for Girls.

By the time I moved into the sixth form, two of my best friends had left. Priscilla left to take up nursing, Peggy's family moved to London, and I stayed on and was elected a prefect. Does "elected" surprise you? When I entered the school an idealistic headmistress called Miss Bedford had instituted a democratic system of self-government. We elected our prefects, we held ballots over such issues as whether to forbid or allow talking in the corridors, and whether the design of the unbecoming pudding-bowl-shaped school cap should be changed. We held brief form meetings on Friday afternoons to discuss form-sized problems. Once, rather bizarrely, the form mistress initiated a discussion on how to help Peggy Llewellin (who was not present) to see that her general attitude was inappropriate. The aim was to do this without being nasty to her, but without encouraging her either (all eyes swivelled to Elaine Floyd as the usual suspect in this regard). I believe some of the mistresses failed to share Miss Bedford's ideals and went through the motions of all this democracy with stony reluctance, and her successor gradually phased them out.

But prefects were still elected in my day. Nobody campaigned to get the job but nobody could avoid the possibility of being landed with it. Not long after I'd been elected I went into one of the cubicles in the lavatory and found someone had written on the wall: "Elaine Floyd is the – prefect in this school." The missing word there is not an expletive. It was either "best" or "worst" and whichever it was had been crossed out; the converse verdict had been written above it and then itself crossed out, so that a line of "best-worst-best-worst" climbed up as far the arms of the scribes could reach. I'm still mystified by that. As a prefect I'd simply gone through the motions, like the other prefects, issuing perfunctory reminders to put the milk bottles back in the crates and things like that. Later in life I got quite accustomed to being treated by some people with warm approval and by others with cold hostility – but at least when that time came, I knew what I'd done to bring it on.

A momentous day arrived. It was St. David's Day. Like the School Play, it was a big event in the calendar. There were prizes for best this and that, and some of the entries were judged by outsiders – including actual *males,* no less, local worthies or school governors, who spoke a few words and handed out the prizes. The writer of the best poem in English (me) was crowned with a coronet of laurel like Julius Caesar, and the writer of the best Welsh poem was chaired, to cries of "*A oes heddwch?*" just as in the National Eisteddfod.

On reaching home, I paused in the passage to remove my school cap and don the laurel wreath before opening the door to break the good news and receive plaudits. The four of them were just sitting there and fell silent as I came in. There was a tension in the room you could cut with a knife. Olive murmured something like "Yes, very good, very nice", but nobody looked at me and nobody smiled. It was as if they wished I'd go back out again, so that whatever was going on could continue to go on.

Apparently someone had called at the house to inform them that one of the pumpsmen at the Great Western Colliery had dropped dead. There would be an opening for a successor, and if Billy was quick off the mark he would have a good chance of getting it, because not many local people had the requisite skills. It would be a steady job and bring in the magnificent sum of four pounds a week. Wasn't that cause for rejoicing?

The problem was that Billy's health was failing. He was then around fifty. Two years previously he'd had an attack of rheumatic fever and been warned against putting strain on his heart. He'd also put on weight, and the long years of smoking had left him wheezy. The job of pumpsman would not be physically exacting as long as nothing went wrong with the ageing machinery, but unlike his previous job of driving the fan it would be carried out underground. Every third weekend when the shifts changed, he'd have a doubler. That meant spending sixteen hours on end at the bottom of the pit, staying awake all through the night with no company except for the small colony of rats – and the pit cat which kept their numbers down, and to that end spent its whole life down there, as the pit ponies did.

He can't have wanted to do that job, but how could he pass up the chance after all those years unemployed? Olive can't have wanted to urge him to take it if he didn't feel up to it, but how could she have helped hoping after all those years that he might think it possible? The outcome concerned them all. It wasn't discussed in front of me so I can only guess who said what. Normally I'd have hated to think what Martha might have said, but that afternoon when I walked in she seemed totally subdued.

Next day Billy went to the pit head and they signed him on.

At first he did nothing but his job, conserving his energies, making sure he was up to it. But after a few months, an old dream that had seemed dead and buried began to stir. There were stretches of time underground when he had nothing much to do but be there: he kept two packs of cards in the pump room to play patience with. Then he took a notebook down too, and his special carpenter's pencil called a bluelead.

Olive, after dealing with the more urgent replacements in the way of worn-out household items, had once begun to save money in a box, which she was careful not to stick a label on in case it might tempt the gods to punish her presumption. The inscription she didn't write on the box would have read "Bathroom??"

Question marks would be necessary, because it was a big undertaking. Before St. David's Day Billy had had time but there wasn't the money. Now that there was the prospect of affording it, the problem was finding the time and the energy. He could only use the hours that should have been leisure hours, and he was older. He had to pace himself, and take rests. By this time he was as fixated on the project as Olive was. He'd had years enough to think about what would be involved. Now he began drawing diagrams, compiling lists, consulting catalogues, taking measurements with his slide rule.

Because he was Billy, this was going to be no ordinary bathroom. It would be unlike any other in the whole world, because the bath would have no proper taps. It would even be a kind of joke. When he proudly led anyone into it to admire it, they would stare and scratch their heads, and say "But – there's no – I mean how do you—? Where does the water come from?" and he could pretend to scratch his head too, and say "Damn, I knew I'd forgotten something."

The biggest bedroom would become the bathroom – bigger than it needed to be, but that was where it would be easiest to plumb it in, so sleeping arrangements were all swapped around and I ended up in the boxroom. The grate had to be taken out together with the oven attached to it, which meant the hub of the house had vanished. For the best part of a week there was nothing there but a great ragged hole in the wall surrounded by naked bricks and rubble and soot. It was possible to sit around the little fireplace in the other room and boil a kettle, but that was it. We ate sandwiches and bought fish and chips. Olive had to grit her teeth and let a Monday go by without changing the sheets.

But it worked. The great day came. The bath was not standing nakedly on claw legs like old-fashioned ones. It was enclosed by a marble-effect partition. The thing that was unique about it was this: it had a hot tap and a cold tap inasmuch as you could turn them on and off, but there was no spout attached to either of them through which water could emerge. It did look very much like an oversight. The secret lay in a lever low down in the partition. You pushed the lever to one side, turned on the taps and water came up from the plughole. You could start with cold and adjust the temperature to your heart's desire and simply wait for it to fill to the required depth. At the end you pushed the lever the other way and the water ran out again. An official came from the Water Board to confirm that it didn't infringe the regulations.

Billy contended that this invention, if patented, could have two advantages. The minor one was that it was perfectly silent. If you were in a flat and working shifts, and someone else was asleep in the next room, there'd be no sound of splashing to wake them up. More pertinently in our case, there was barely any steam in the room. In winter, steam would not mist up the mirror or condense on the cold outer walls and trickle down in streams, as in ordinary common-or-garden bathrooms.

I have gone into some detail about this because the stock caricature of miners in those days was that it was a waste of money building houses for them with bathrooms in, since they weren't interested in cleanliness and would only use them for keeping the coal in. I was given the privilege of being the first person to try it out. It was bliss. You could lie down and soak in it. You could stretch your legs out and close your eyes. They were waiting for me to come down and report how it felt.

"Like a film star."

Billy nodded and turned to his ol'ooman.

"Now your turn," he said.

CHAPTER 5

Oxford

I was entered for Oxford rather in the way that a promising horse is entered for the Grand National, without consulting the horse. Personally I had some misgivings. One or two boys from the area had gone down that route and the word got around that you could be pretty lonely and miserable there if you didn't manage to fit in.

Up to form six I'd been leaning towards science, but it was now decided I'd have more of a chance to shine in English. The problem was that my O-levels in chemistry, physics and biology would be irrelevant, whereas Latin and at least one modern language would be essential if I was to be eligible to apply. That sounded okay. I had Latin and Welsh. But Oxford pursed its lips and declared that Welsh was not a modern language (a debatable view, I still maintain) and I was told to mug up some French in my spare time and get an O-level in that. The project was going to involve a lot of hard work. Did I really want to do it?

Some boys from the area had run that course, but there were no role models from the girls' schools. For the boys, education was their best hope of not ending up down the pit. But there was a general feeling that higher education would be wasted on girls because they only end up getting married.

Not only all the Hollywood films but most of the immortal works of literature were unanimous about what constituted a happy-ever-after denouement for a female. And at seventeen I had not yet – as they used to say – given up hope.

Shortly after becoming eighteen, I received a letter from a boy. By post, with a stamp on, and from a boy I'd never met. Well, that goes without saying – I wasn't socially on speaking terms with any of that subdivision of the human race. It was written by the Head Boy of the Pontypridd Intermediate Boys' School and addressed to me in my capacity of Head Girl. It conveyed the news that the joint sixth form dance, traditionally held every other year under the auspices of the staff of both institutions, had been arbitrarily discontinued.

The letter-writer – his name was Graham – proposed to organise such an event off his own bat, as a free citizen, and it would strengthen his hand if I gave this proposal my support. We and two or three others could form a committee, meet in a café, and organise the hire of a venue, sale of tickets, etc. Wonderful! Cinderella shall go to the ball! Clearly it was a far cry from the event at which Elizabeth Bennett first met Mr. Darcy. It wouldn't even be like the cancelled event, which would have taken place in the vast Assembly Hall of the Girls' School. It had to be held in a kind of drill-hall, rather small and low-ceilinged and a bit dingy, but affordable at the price we fixed for the tickets. One respectable older character had agreed to act as Master of Ceremonies and a stand-in for the adult world.

The committee only met twice. The boys were friendly and I had high hopes of getting to know others when the time arrived, so that I'd be able to walk down Taff Street and pass the time of day with boys that I'd danced with and laughed with and drunk lemonade with, just as Audrey and Grace and the others did, and when they talked about Tom and Alan and John I would know who they meant.

The great day arrived. At one end of the room was a bench where you could sit when you weren't dancing, and that was where I spent the evening. I danced twice, both times with the M. C. who saw it as part of his duty to take pity on the wallflowers. I kept on smiling. I chatted brightly to the girls who perched there, breathless and fanning themselves while waiting for the music to start up again. And the iron entered into my soul.

There was no malice involved. They were all having a lovely time with the people they'd come with – I hadn't quite realised you were supposed to come *with* somebody – and they were scheming about how to attract the attention of whoever they hoped to go home with, and I was somehow not part of that process but part of the furniture. I must have been doing something wrong. If we are talking Pride and Prejudice I was Mary Bennett, God help me. And in that capacity I have delighted you long enough, so we'll skip the rest of the proceedings. I walked back to Hopkinstown alone in the dark and the rain, went straight to bed and cried into my pillow for half an hour.

I then turned it over, damp side down, and said to hell with it. At least it clarified the options. I won't pretend the anguish didn't return and have to be driven away on several subsequent occasions, but it got easier with practice. All that, all that stuff that makes the world go round and the poets sing, obviously called for some talent that I was deficient in, but so what? There's a big wide world out there and a hundred other things to do that are just as absorbing. The thing is to find out what they are, and Oxford sounded like a good place to start looking. A generation later the words "fish" and "bicycle" would have sprung to mind, but it was thirty years too early for that.

Anyway, I awoke ready to fix my sights seriously on the Oxford initiative proposed by the headmistress Miss Jenkins. She had done some research and targeted Lady Margaret Hall as the college to aim at. There was a form to fill in, and she suggested I go through a dummy run before completing it, by writing my intended answers on a piece of paper. She was horrified to find that in response to a question about religious affiliation I'd written: "None." (LMH has a strong Anglican tradition.). But what was her objection? Was I supposed to tell lies?

She brushed aside any question of discussing this as an ethical issue, and stuck to the semantics of words like affiliate. They weren't enquiring about the current state of my soul – they just wanted to know where I was coming from. She asked about my family and pounced: "There you are – brought up Baptist. That's all they're looking for. Put Baptist." She convinced me that "None" would have looked like flaunting my lack of faith and give the impression of aggressiveness and bad manners. It was a cop-out but I went along with it.

I was invited to Oxford for an interview at Lady Margaret Hall which involved staying overnight and getting a look at the place. One of the mistresses tactfully enquired what I would be wearing, and since we were the same size wondered whether I might wish to consider borrowing a dress. It was a good dress, very well made and perfectly suited to the occasion. I got off the train at Oxford station and failed to register that some of the vehicles standing outside were taxis. They were outside my ken.

A bus took me to Carfax but there was still a long trek out to Norham Gardens and I was grateful to a woman who kindly suggested I put my suitcase onto the pram she was pushing. Prams in those days were high and capacious. Hearing that I was going to LMH for an interview she assured me it would be a walkover. They were glad to get hold of anybody these days, she said, owing to the number of girls going off to work in factories, where the money was better. She had naturally assumed I was being interviewed for a job as a maid. That rubbed off some of the confidence that the borrowed dress had inspired.

However, all went well. I was interviewed by the Principal and I remember only three things about it. One was the long, long walk from the door of her room to where she sat at the other end of it. Another was her favourable mention of my proficiency in Latin – I had an A-level distinction in it and I suppose it was quite an Oxfordish thing to be good at. The third impression was how quickly it was over. I think the fact is they just want to take a look at you, take in the voice and the body language and so on, and see if you'll do. The verdict was favourable. I was awarded an exhibition from the college, and a grant from Glamorgan County Council, and I was in.

A few days before I went up to Oxford, two things happened. War was declared, and Billy went into hospital. I had been too self-absorbed in the last few months to notice that everything had become an effort for him. I didn't know that he had taken to coming home down the back lane rather than the street, so that people wouldn't notice how often he had to stop and lean against the wall to get his breath back. He was fifty-two. When the ambulance arrived I went with him to the front door and he stopped in the passage and put an arm round me and gave me a hug. I couldn't remember that he'd ever done that before.

All through my first term at Oxford while he was in hospital I wrote to him, knowing that Olive would read the letters when she visited. He liked getting the letters in the envelopes with the crest on – "*Dominus Illuminatio Mea*" – and I wrote every day and he answered once a week. The last one he wrote ended "Yours temporarily grumpy but not for long". He was right about that. A telegram arrived at college two days before I was supposed to sit for Pass Mods and they said I should go home and could take the exam in the spring instead.

After the funeral, the women sitting around in the house told Olive that now that she was a widow I must certainly leave Oxford and get a job and help out, because the widow's pension was only ten shillings a week. But her response was "Over my dead body". The last thing she wanted was for me to chuck it in. Instead she took in lodgers – young rookie policemen because she felt she could depend on their being respectable characters.

Chucking it in was the last thing I wanted too. I was loving it there. I'd entered the place trying to equip myself with mental armour of stoical indifference in case I couldn't cope, but it turned out to be quite unnecessary. I've been re-reading an account of the Oxford experience of the novelist Gwyn Thomas a few years earlier, trying to understand why he hated it there.

Most of the books about pre-war Oxford are about male Oxford, and the protagonists had either been to public schools or were harassed and persecuted by the majority that *had* attended them. The men's colleges were in most cases very ancient and sticklers for tradition, but the women's colleges were comparatively new, set up in the teeth of those traditions. No ivy clothed their walls. Women had still not been admitted to membership of the Oxford Union, and in some of the lectures we attended, alpha male dons pointedly addressed their mixed audiences as "Gentlemen". It's true that any trace of suffragette militancy was dead and gone, but everyone there had chosen to be there and worked hard to get there. In that respect they constituted a minority to which I belonged as of right.

Another reason why I was not unduly embarrassed by my surroundings might be that I was a bit obtuse. Some of the things I said and did may well have – make that "must have" – set their teeth on edge. But they didn't express these feelings by debagging me and throwing me into a fountain, as sometimes happened in the men's colleges, nor even (as would have happened back home) by saying "I wish to God you'd stop doing that."

The signals they used to convey these things to one another – slight alterations to the intonation or the angle of an eyebrow – were so minimal and delicate that unless you'd been brought up to read them they were invisible. In top people's magazines the agony columns often printed letters complaining of the habits of, say, a new sister-in-law, and enquiring "How can I convey to her that this makes us all feel uncomfortable?" The solution "Try telling her" had never occurred to the letter writer, and was seldom proffered by the counsellor.

Anyway, with only one or two exceptions they were always polite and often very kind. One did murmur that I was "geysh", which I found puzzling, but then I worked out that she was trying to say "gauche". I was comforted by the knowledge that though her English accent was more refined than mine, her French one was appalling.

Quite soon though I made some good friends – Ursula, and Ruth, and Marion, and Clarissa – and they remained friends for life. We could and did talk for hours about anything and everything. We shared enough basic values to make any differences in outlook interesting but in the end unimportant. So I was certainly never lonely there. The place was beautiful, the workload was light, and I began to believe I belonged there.

It was in Oxford, oddly enough, that I became politicised. You'd think it would have happened sooner. Politics in the valleys was passionate, pervasive, and radical. It was suffused with a faith in the future that sustained some sense of confidence and self-worth in the community as a whole even through the worst times, which would otherwise be very hard to explain. But it was 99% male and about 95% dominated by the miners' union. There were no members of that union in our house, and consequently politics never cropped up as a topic of discussion.

Just around that time, the Labour Club in Oxford had been

infiltrated by Communist entryism to the point of take-over, and the dissident moderates were driven to setting up their own outfit, the Democratic Socialist Club, led by a pair of highly talented young men, who both later became leading lights in the Labour Party and cabinet ministers in the post-war Government.

The first chairman was Tony Crosland. He was tall, handsome, charismatic, with romantic hair and a mellifluous voice, and whereas everybody else had bikes, he tootled around Oxford in a little red car. In the following term the chairman was Roy Jenkins, whose long spell as Home Secretary was to introduce so many long-overdue reforms. By the fourth term the chairman of that club was me, and that takes some explaining.

I wasn't leadership material. I was reading English, and debates about economic issues like Exchange Control went right over my head. The main reason I moved up through the ranks was the call-up. The undergraduates who would normally have taken over were being conscripted in their second year to be trained as officers in the armed forces. I was a member of the club's committee, dutifully carrying out any jobs assigned to me, and had written one or two pieces for the Oxford Socialist. Maybe there were two other rivals vying for leadership and my name slipped through the middle as a compromise candidate – I don't know. I never canvassed for it. It was bit like being elected Head Girl, but it never occurred to me to back away from it.

One person who was exasperated by this turn of events was Professor G. D. H. Cole, who enjoyed acting as a kind of *eminence grise*, grooming the young hopefuls for future high office. For serious career politicians he was there to offer guidance, provide contacts, pull strings, and by acting as their mentor, influence the future of the Labour Party and potentially of the entire country. He was intelligent and high-principled and knowledgeable and had good contacts and did a lot of good work for the cause.

I was young, educable, eager to please and could have used some guidance, but he'd been against my election, seeing it a complete waste of time when the experience would have been helpful for some future statesman. Feeling insulted by the outcome when I was elected anyway, he went back into his tent like Achilles and simply waited for this term to be over and the club to come back to its senses.

I made no attempt to be an indoctrinator, since I wasn't qualified for that. I took it that I'd been elected by the members and for the members – to keep the show on the road and get hold of some good speakers that they could listen to and make up their own minds. I booked people like Susan Lawrence, a member of the Labour Party executive and in her earlier days a doughty fighter for women's suffrage, and Kingsley Martin, editor of the New Statesman. The most impressive name on my list was that of the Home Secretary, Herbert Morrison.

That was liable to be a tricky meeting. He had recently banned the Daily Worker (Stalin had just made a pact with Hitler) and expressed the hope that there would not be "trouble." I recognised a bunch of people at the back with steam to blow off on this topic. When the time came for questions, I picked three of them in a row. Since they'd all been primed with questions on the Daily Worker issue, to be fed in at regular intervals, the last one was greeted with groans of boredom and I was then able to observe mildly that since the questions so far seemed to have been variations on a single theme, perhaps we might now move on to a different one? It worked, and Morrison afterwards congratulated me on the way I'd handled the situation.

Halfway through the term I conceived a bright idea. The country was by now stiff with refugees from Hitler, including a number of Socialist activists from different countries that had been over-run. Could we invite a selection of them to Oxford and put them up for a weekend, to meet one another and exchange ideas and experiences with each other and with us? I approached G. D. H. Cole and asked if he could suggest names that should be on the list. He stared at me and gave an unsmiling one-syllable answer: "No." The event took place nevertheless, and received a shot in the arm from a contribution by Professor Harold Laski. My invitation to him had been a long shot, but he turned up and made a memorable speech that has stuck in my mind from that day to this, identifying one of the drawbacks of unrestricted capitalism as the creation of hyper-urbanised nation states suffering from "apoplexy at the centre and anaemia at the extremities."

All in all, the proceedings during that term lacked some of the gravitas the club had been accustomed to, but I don't think it harmed the cause. The activities were quite lively. And the membership went up. I've gone into this at some length because it looks like one of the experiences that we are meant to learn from. Maybe I should have learned never to punch above my weight, but to lie low until I could be sure of commanding respectful attention. But I think life is too short. If you wait for that, unless you start out bearing the hallmarks of "one of us", you could wait forever.

One day in the following term while walking along the pavement I was accosted by Drummond Allison. I'd never met him before. He said he was planning to go for a walk with his friend Christopher Tosswill. It would be a long day out, they'd be taking sandwiches and he invited me to go with them. Well, why not? We walked a long way, we both did a lot of talking and Christopher got a few words in edgeways, and by the time we got back Drummond was outlining a list of other places that I really ought to be shown. We could go to the botanical gardens, we could visit Pope's tower in Stanton Harcourt…

On the face of it we had nothing in common. Drummond came from the kind of background where he was brought up by a nurse, called his mother Mater and his father "sir", went to a prep school and Bishop Stortford College, and was mad about cricket. His father was a chartered accountant and his mother, of Viennese extraction, had been a lady-in-waiting. He did have some broadly left-wing views and had friends who were Communists: at that time and place it was the thing to be and for a while even Iris Murdoch seemed to be heading that way. But Drummond was the opposite of any kind of politician.

He was essentially a poet. He was one of the "Eight Oxford Poets" who'd recently published a book of that title which had received some good reviews. They included his close friends Sidney Keys and John Heath-Stubbs, who tended to refer to the rival group of Oxford poets centring around Philip Larkin and Kingsley Amis as "the Audenists". Drummond however said of his own group "they were so beastly to Auden that I definitely took him under my protection."

It's not easy to see quite why we instantly got on so well. I suppose a headful of English Literature provided some common basis, and there was shared enthusiasm for some particular writers. James Thurber was one. But the keynote was Camelot. I'd just read and loved "The Sword in the Stone", and Drummond was steeped in all that because T. H. White was a friend of his family, went on holidays to Cornwall with them, and had told Drummond the stories about Arthur and Merlin, and drawn him pictures of the magical animals, long before they went into the book.

Perhaps what we recognised in each other was a kind of immaturity. It felt a bit like that. We'd both had an only-child kind of upbringing – he had brothers, but they were much older – and that may foster a tendency to construct private mental worlds and be reluctant to complete the metamorphosis into the prosaic and responsible phase of existence that is supposed to follow. We spent a lot of time together, knowing it would be brief because he was due to move on to Sandhurst.

Something bizarre happened to delay that. He was in a play, acting the part of a young Communist who ended up being bullied and pistol-whipped, and the action became so realistic that there was blood all over the stage. The audience was left to surmise that the producer had gone a bit over the top with the tomato sauce or whatever, but after the curtain fell Drummond was taken into the Radcliffe Infirmary. By misadventure a small artery in his skull had been severed, and his call-up was deferred.

The delay irked him. He wasn't looking forward to the possibility of being killed – who would be? But he also had complicated worries about being seen not to be brave enough when it came to the crunch. T. H. White had a line about Lancelot : "He felt in his heart cruelty and cowardice, the things that made him brave and kind." Exams were over. His friends were dispersing, mostly into the armed forces. He didn't want to go home, nor to stay alone in Oxford. He asked me stay on into the long vacation.

Was this "the real thing"? The question has no relevance. There was a war on. There was plenty of amorous dalliance but neither of us used the word "love" or saw the prospect of travelling the road of life together side by side and on into the sunset. That would certainly never have worked out. To borrow a phrase from the sixties, I was somebody who at that difficult time made him feel all right. He made me feel all right too. From then on I ceased to suspect that there was some basic defect in me that I just had to learn to live with.

When he passed out at Sandhurst as an officer, he invited me down to watch the ceremony – there was nobody else able and willing to attend. In 1943 he was killed in the assault on Monte Camino. He died bravely – he needn't have worried about that. In 1994 I was invited to his old school to the launch of a book of his collected poems, including the ones he wrote to me. His mother had died by then, but other members of his family were there, and so was John Heath-Stubbs, the only survivor of that Oxford trio. In the seventies, a magazine review of the poetry of the forties selected Drummond as "perhaps the most absorbed and striking elegist of Auden's 'low dishonest decade'."

Somebody else called him a life-enhancer. I'd go along with that.

CHAPTER 6

Norfolk

In my last term at Oxford, two head-hunters came to the college to ask permission to try to interest some third-year students in the idea of working in Adult Education in East Anglia. At that time there was a particularly strong flavour of idealism in the prospect of delivering a chance of acquiring learning and culture to men and women who'd had to leave school early and regretted it.

The two men who came were Frank Jaques and John Hampden Jackson. Frank gave the impression of having risen from the ranks and being keen to inspire others to do the same. But J. H. J. had the accent of the upper crust and I was told – by a Fabian who was his contemporary – that in his youth he'd been one of the public schoolboys who had volunteered as strikebreakers by driving buses during the National Strike. He certainly wasn't right wing, but he had his own rarefied philosophical stance. He was passionately in favour of the common people. I don't know whether or not he was descended from the East Anglian rebel leader John Hampden, the cousin of Oliver Cromwell who died in battle against the Royalists, but he was quite happy to share his name.

However, the workers he was really devoted to were the tillers and hedgers and ditchers, the smiths and carpenters and saddlers of the England of yore. It would be much harder to imagine him working up quite the same enthusiasm for the proletariat of Birmingham, Slough, or Liverpool. He himself led the simple life with no frills and almost no mod cons, in an old farmhouse near Wymondham with his wife and four children. He was a first class educator and inspirer, with bags of charisma, and did a great job of convincing the East Anglians who attended his classes that they were the salt of the earth. That can't be a bad thing to do for people, wherever you do it.

In peace time these organisers would have applied to one of the men's colleges for recruits, but conscription had changed all that, so they booked three alumni of Lady Margaret Hall to commence work in September 1942. Of the other two, Grace was the daughter of the Dean of St. Albans, and Diana later became a star turn in the campaign for the ordination of women in the Church of England. The arrangement was that every winter, each of us would settle for six months in a particular spot – Norwich, say, or Wells – and from there conduct five weekly evening courses, in five villages accessible from that spot, one on each night of the week.

"Accessible" was an elastic term. Britain had been at war for three years, and transport, like food and clothes, was rationed. There was no petrol for non-essential motoring. On the railways the movement of troops and materiel had priority. The civilian population was admonished by posters and officials demanding "Is your journey really necessary?"

Besides, some of the villages were not on the railway anyway. One or two in my schedule involved a five or six mile bicycle ride to the venue, and either a ride back in the blackout, or overnight accommodation in the home of some member of the class. I remember being stopped in a country lane one night by a policeman because my bicycle contravened the blackout regulations by not having an adequate mask over the headlamp. He let me off with a caution, not knowing that I already had form in this connection: in Oxford I'd been fined ten shillings for the opposite offence – cruising back to college five minutes after lighting-up time with no lamp at all. ("Hatless in court", ran the headline in the Oxford Mail. "Oxford mayor reprimands undergraduate.")

So it was often easier to stay overnight, and people were generous in opening their homes to the tutors. I never forget staying with Mr. and Mrs. Quantrell. In Norfolk the east wind blows straight from the Urals, with no intervening high ground to slow it down – but they had a real feather bed. You could step into an icy bedroom with your teeth chattering, climb into that bed and in quite a short time be as warm as toast.

The trains, though often overcrowded, usually ran on time. Once on the way back to base I fell asleep and was carried on to the terminus at Great Yarmouth. I wandered around in the rain and the blackout, walked into the crowded bar of a hotel and asked for a room. The barmaid said that that end of the business only operated in the summer season. I wandered further, found a police station, and enquired if they had a cell where I could lay my head for the night. A constable escorted me back to the hotel, and pronounced that since it advertised itself as a residential establishment, I had the legal right to ask to reside there. It wasn't the barmaid's fault, since she could hardly leave her post untended, but she gave me a key to one of the bedrooms. The sheets were unaired and the blankets inadequate but in 1942 one slogan covered all such inconveniences: "Don't you know there's a war on?"

The work itself, if you can call it that, I thoroughly enjoyed. It consisted of talking to people about things I was interested in for about forty minutes in the evening, and then spending at least an equivalent amount of time listening to them and learning from their ideas and experiences. J. H. J. in one of his books commented that trying to understand current affairs could be like walking into a cinema halfway through a film, with no-one to tell you who the characters were or how they got into the predicament they seemed to be wrestling with. Our job was filling in that background. In Oxford my primary job was supposed to be studying English Literature, so my knowledge of recent history and current affairs was limited, but in Norfolk I had all day long to read up about some chosen – or requested – aspect of it, and if anyone asked a question I couldn't answer, I had no difficulty in admitting it, and promising to try to find the answer by the following week. It was money for jam. I was deliriously happy doing that job and couldn't believe my luck.

Three factors contributed to that feeling. For one thing, there was the great and blessed difference between teaching adults and teaching children: nobody was there that didn't want to be there. And there was a much more urgent thirst for knowledge then. Today, with a certain amount of channel-switching on tv and web-surfing on a pc, you can feel comfortably au fait with English history, the natural world, the Roman Empire, geology, foreign countries, and the achievements of famous figures from the past, without having to go out and sit in a draughty schoolroom to hear about them.

Sixty years ago, ignorance of such things was thicker and blacker and more constricting. In cities and industrial areas there were libraries and Mechanics' Institutes and informed discussion, but deep in the countryside there was next to nothing. In the smaller villages people sometimes turned up who weren't conscious of wanting to learn, just because wartime conditions had left those places even more cut off from the world, and simply having a new voice to listen to once a week constituted an event.

Country people are often portrayed as taciturn. I never found that. They had plenty to say, and there was plenty they had thought about, but they had had no one to say it to who wanted to listen. Only one thing could shut them up like clams. The major difference between Norfolk and back home was that the Welsh coalfields were virtually classless. (Kingsley Amis, after living in Swansea, used that word for them.) Valleys people knew that there were rich people who owned the mines and controlled their lives, but they lived elsewhere. You would never pass one of them in the street. But sometimes in Norfolk, once or twice in a term, a local person of consequence – male, or female, or occasionally a married couple – would drop into a class out of benign curiosity, or to check up on what was going on in their parish. They would helpfully contribute one or two pertinent comments on the subject matter, but while they were there nobody else would say a word. Those discussion periods were like wading through treacle. All that must have changed by now. It was a very long time ago.

One day I was walking on a road beside a railway track and a train passed by with American soldiers hanging out of the windows, waving and shouting greetings like "Hiya, Blahndie!" Since there was no other female in sight I thought they must have been a long time in transit, and I'd been symbolically promoted into blonde-hood, so I waved back. From the point of view of the war effort we certainly had every reason to be glad they'd arrived. Pretty soon they were everywhere, because Norfolk, being flat and not too far from Europe, was an ideal place for building airfields.

They could constitute something of a hazard on the evenings when I got back late to Norwich around pub closing time. I remember being backed into a corner by a G. I. who assumed that any lone female walking the streets in the blackout must ipso facto be a streetwalker, and tried to plunge his hand down what he confidently expected would be my *décolletage*. On encountering a garment buttoned up to the neck and secured with a brooch, he uttered an incredulous question: "A peee-yun?" Clearly then not a hooker, he decided, and perhaps even somebody's sister, so like the well-brought-up Southern boy he doubtless was, he apologised and gave me a couple of there-there pats, and went off in search of better luck next time.

I only got to know one of them – not a blondie-hailer, but a quiet American, a bookish New Yorker called Irwin Rosenzweig. Sometimes we'd go out for fish and chips and a movie on a Saturday. I wonder if he's still alive? We lost contact and I never even knew whether he survived the war. The first time he called for me at the little house I was lodging in, he politely asked the landlady if he could use the bathroom and she said there wasn't one. I'll never forget their expressions of mutual disbelief. He couldn't believe that even Brits could live in houses with no indoor plumbing, and she couldn't believe a strange man would demand to take a bath when he'd only been in the house for fifteen minutes.

In Norfolk the adult education syllabus only lasted from September to March, so in the summers I could do something different, as I had got into the habit of doing during the long vac while at Oxford. One summer, for instance, I had felt an urge to experience London. At that time there were occasional air raids there as elsewhere, but the real London Blitz had not yet begun. I arrived there like any other immigrant with very little money and no contacts, so I grabbed the first job I saw advertised, to give myself time to look for a better one. The first job was washing dishes in the deep shelter underneath Berkeley Square. Residence in such a prestigious address didn't guarantee that the Germans wouldn't drop bombs on you, but it did entitle you, while underground, to a decent amount of space and headroom and a decent meal to tuck into while awaiting the all clear.

More often, though, I tended to stay home in the summer and take a local job, for example as progress chaser in a sparking plug factory. Wherever I was, I spent less that I earned – which wasn't difficult since I'd never been in a position to acquire expensive tastes – and gave the balance to Olive.

She was always glad of it but insisted on treating these contributions as a windfall and earning her own living in various ways. At one point she was instructed to take in an evacuee – a boy called Peter, who wore leg-irons because he'd been a victim of polio. She was surprised to find that his father intended coming with him. He was anxious about the boy because of his disability, and was himself disoriented because his wife had just walked out on both of them, so he found a job in a local factory – they were always crying out for labour – and he and Peter stayed on there together for a year or so. Then they revisited London one weekend in the hope of patching up the marriage, and were both killed outright in an air raid.

One year when I came home from Norfolk, Olive had been offered a three-days-a-week job in the wages department of Simmons Aerocessories factory in Treforest, and was anxious to take it. Her mother Martha got into a bit of a flutter at the thought of being left in sole charge of the house for part of the day. The solution was for me to take over the minimal role of stand-in housekeeper during the running-in period, until Martha saw how easy and possible it was.

I can't claim to have been very good at it. When I was growing up I hadn't been allowed to do anything in the domestic line – any more than if I'd been a boy – except cleaning the knives and forks on a Friday, and occasionally the windows. I did my best and even began to take some pride in this new skill, but I didn't really pass muster. Olive would sometimes come home and run a finger along an undusted ledge. When I became ambitious and made a rhubarb tart because rhubarb was cheap and in season, the result was palatable but she worried about the amount of sugar involved. She'd garnered a stash of it against a possible rainy day when the rations might be even tighter than they were then, and she was afraid I was using it up as if there was no tomorrow.

During that interlude I went out one evening to attend a 'Beds for Stalingrad' rally in Pontypridd. Among the panel of speakers, the star turn was a young man from Ynysybwl who'd fought in Spain with the International Brigade and been a prisoner of war in one of Franco's jails. When he was released in an exchange of prisoners, he'd been given a welcome home parade with accompanying brass band, and was now teaching French in the Pontypridd Boys' Grammar School.

Nobody at that stage of the war could overstate the sufferings of the Russian people, the appalling scale of their losses, or the fact that the Red Army, by putting up a more determined resistance than any other army in Europe, was giving Britain a breathing space. It was giving us time to tool up and prepare for the time when Hitler might, as he planned, have defeated Russia and would be free to concentrate all his forces on the invasion and subjection of these islands. The Russians were our indispensable allies and 'Beds for Stalingrad' the best of good causes.

All the same, as the meeting progressed, I got a bit restive at the way that the courage of the Russian people was being identified with and attributed to the virtues of the Stalinist recipe for running a country. I felt the two things should be kept distinct. When somebody came round collecting written and signed questions to be put to the panel, I handed in a couple of queries on those lines. As they were read out I heard one or two people asking who (the hell) I was. I'd been away a long time and there were only two or three people there that I recognised.

The following day I was scrubbing the floor of the glasshouse when Martha answered the doorbell and came in looking seriously flustered. There was a young man at the door asking to see me: what was she to say? I said tell him to come in. But where was she to put him? She meant that I was in no state to receive gentleman callers. Her instinct was to side-track him into the front room while I darted upstairs to change and do something about my hair. I said look, it doesn't matter, tell him to come in.

Enter Morien Morgan.

CHAPTER 7

Morien

It was, of course, the commie French master who'd been on the platform the previous evening. He was tall and dark (tall was rare in South Wales) and I liked the sound of his voice. I think I've always been more attuned to the way people sound than the way they look.

He didn't have much in the way of the social graces – he sat down opposite me, ignoring Martha once she'd let him in, and said we ought to talk, but not here. Perhaps we could meet in Pontypridd for a coffee one evening. Say seven o'clock in the café in Mill Street? Say tonight or tomorrow? I assumed his intention was to point out the errors in my thinking, and I'm always game to let anybody have a go at that if they're feeling lucky. Sometimes I'm wrong and they're right, and then I've learned something. So I said okay, let's say tomorrow. When he got up to go, he did remember to say thank you to Martha for the cup of tea that she'd put into his hand and which he'd wordlessly accepted, in the way males in the valleys accepted most things that were done for them, as part of the natural order of things.

I'd better fill in something about his background. He came from Ynysybwl, one of the dead-end coal-mining valleys like the Rhondda and the Cynon which converge at the commercial centre of Pontypridd. His father was Johnny Morgan, a shining example of the stuff that working-class heroes were made of at that time. He was checkweighman at the colliery (a sort of tribune ensuring fair play when the men's drams were assessed for payment) and the long-standing secretary of the Lady Windsor Lodge of the miners' union. There were certainly no perks for union officials then – quite the reverse. His best friend was blacklisted and hounded from the valley for union activity. Johnny himself was often denounced by the owners, but escaped victimisation because he was 100% non-violent. When disputes threatened to turn nasty and lead to attacks on blacklegs or destruction of property, his was the only voice that could take the heat out of the situation.

He was self-educated, and widely read, and had written and published a history of industrial relations in that valley entitled "A Village Workers' Council," which later drew words of praise in a letter from the then head of the Coal Board – Professor Jacob Bronowski, no less. Johnny was no chapel-goer. In one of Wales's recurrent religious revivals, his mother and sisters had literally gone down on their knees in the kitchen imploring him to come to Jesus, without success. But he had all the non-conformist virtues of uprightness and abstinence and continence and reliability. In the eyes of his wife, Maggie, he was incorruptible to a fault. During the long strike when the miners were organising soup-kitchens, she didn't see why she had to go and queue up with the other wives when he could so easily have brought their fair share of the food home with him. But justice must not only be done: it must be seen to be done. And Maggie had to queue, with everybody else.

So according to the standards of that time and place, Morien had been born of the blood royal. He was only fulfilling his destiny when after a somewhat cynical youth misspent in billiard halls he heard the call to arms while he was a student at Cardiff University and rose to the occasion by enlisting in the International Brigade.

He was the youngest of five. His birth had not been a cause for unmixed rejoicing, especially by his mother. She had previously borne four children and since the last one had endured a stillbirth with severe complications from which she had taken months to recover, and she had begun to hope that all that kind of thing was over and done with. Gwyn Thomas, who was the youngest of twelve, once wrote a line that moved me to tears, saying that his mother "sometimes looked at me as if she could almost forgive me for being there." Morien – with how much justification I don't know – believed that in his own case such forgiveness had barely been forthcoming.

In two important respects his upbringing had resembled mine. For his first six or seven years his health too had given cause for anxiety, so like me he'd often stayed indoors while his contemporaries were being sent out to play and learning to get on with one another. The other thing we had in common was being passed as infants from lap to lap and constantly being talked to and stimulated, because his two elder sisters doted on their youngest baby brother. He too learned to read before he ever went to school. He started school even later than I did, partly because of an accident that had left him blind in one eye. Chance circumstances like these may put a kind of kink in your relationships with other people: it was rare to meet somebody who had had similar experiences.

In the café in Pontypridd, Morien ordered two coffees and lit a cigarette, and within ten minutes it felt as if we were picking up where we'd left off on some previous occasion, except that there hadn't been a previous occasion. The ostensible agenda for the meeting was the exchange of views in the field of current affairs. Readers of romantic disposition may wince and think: "What are they doing? No good can come of this. At their age it should have been poetry, not politics."

The forgotten thing is that there have been times and places where the two things came together. Think Wordsworth, Shelley, Byron, Burns. They all made music out of the dream of the brotherhood of man. When they wrote things like "Bliss was it in that dawn to be alive, and to be young was very heaven", they weren't referring to the rosy hues of sunrise, but to political events on the continent of Europe. Before long there was poetry too. Morien was very well versed in the works of the Romantics in both French and English, and phrases from them seeped into the first letter he ever wrote to me. It was nineteen pages long.

That was still the 1940s and political correctness hadn't been invented, and he was still unreconstructed by today's standards. He was Marxist enough to hold that all human beings have equal rights, but he had got hold of the idea – commoner then, but by no means dead today – that women through no fault of their own, poor things, are unable to think straight. He gradually came to accept that there may be exceptions to that rule, and it was reassuring that he was pleased about it. So many males find intelligence in women a total turn-off. In those days, even in the small change of everyday life, in interactions with strangers, it could seem gratuitously aggressive, unfeminine, an unprovoked attack on a man's self-esteem, for a woman to say to him: "Are you sure about that?" let alone "Well, I think that's rubbish." It was relaxingly safe to say rubbish to Morien. He might laugh, but he wouldn't wilt.

Predictably, the course of true love didn't run smooth. For one thing, there was Olive. From the moment they met, he didn't like my mother and she didn't like him. Most people liked her – what was not to like? Most male people in particular were putty in her hands, but not Morien. She was thankful that it was getting near the end of summer, and before very long I'd be far away in Norfolk out of harm's way. Six months apart would give ample opportunity for both of us to meet up with somebody more suitable. That didn't work out though. Morien applied for, and secured, a new job in the boys' grammar school at Swaffham in Norfolk, and we spent most weekends together from then on.

Over Christmas he announced to his startled family that he intended to marry the girl from Hopkinstown whom they'd met once briefly before he went to Swaffham. I liked his mother, Maggie. She wasn't charming but she was irrepressibly outspoken and she made me laugh. I don't think she had any personal dislike for me, but she did take me aside and warn me that Morien was "not strong." The implication was that if I was looking for a good provider to look after me in the long years ahead, I might do better elsewhere. I listened solemnly and said I'd take that risk.

Her reasons for this were financial. Morgan economics were based on the principle that every child must be given all the education it could absorb. Having done that, he/she was then expected to stay unmarried and contribute to the family budget long enough to complete the education of the next in line. Morien had no younger siblings to subsidise, but Maggie had reckoned that after wasting a couple of years wandering off to Spain and all that nonsense, he'd now stay single for a few more years to repay what had been invested in him. However, he was the least biddable of her children and she wasn't going to tangle with him.

It was harder on Olive. Billy had always predicted that I'd end up marrying "some fellow from the two foot nine" (that's the narrowest seam in the colliery). But she had wanted so much for me to shine. She'd have been very proud and happy if I'd stayed single and become a headmistress. She'd have been perfectly content if I'd married into a posh family that would have looked down on her – it would have been enough that I'd bettered myself. She'd have settled, less happily, for a run-of-the-mill son-in-law if only he would have teased and hugged her and sworn that he'd mistaken her for my sister. But she couldn't bear that after all that wasted education I was going to end up washing Morien's socks. She couldn't understand him, nor what I saw in him. I wished heartily for her sake that it could have been different, and it was a long-running grief to me. But that's life. Martha had been equally appalled by Billy and his disrespect and godlessness and silly vulgar jokes, but he was the one Olive wanted, and Martha couldn't win either.

One point needs to be made about that wasted education: I never for a second saw it in that light, either then or later. Education is never wasted. The idea that I'd been swept off my feet, side-tracked from the highroad to a glittering career and into the cul-de-sac of marriage – that was miles off the mark. In those days there was no way of "having it all" unless you were rich. The traditional division of labour made perfect sense in the stage of technology that then existed, because unless you were rich, bringing up a family was necessarily a full-time job. You couldn't even be a teacher in an infants' school without knowing that you would be instantly slung out if you got married. Choices had to be made. In the words of the old Spanish proverb: "Take what you want, said God. And pay for it." I knew what I wanted, and the price tag was clearly attached, and it was okay with me. I had not been sure that I would get it though, because it takes two to tango.

As it turned out, the tango was one of Morien's more unforeseen accomplishments. He took me a staff dance at the boys' grammar school where he turned out to be a quite unexpectedly good dancer, and I met his colleagues. On his own ground he came over as witty, popular, stimulating, decisive, dependable. I soon learned how much the boys liked him too, especially the backward ones. He put his heart into teaching them. He opened up vistas for them. All my life I've had people come up to me and say "He taught my son" or "He taught me" or "My father still talks about him." Often it's spoken of as a memorable thing, a turning point. I once met a Scot who'd been with him in Franco's jail at San Pedro, and he told me how Morien did more than anyone else to keep their spirits up, even through the worst times.

Nevertheless, people on both sides were privately advising caution. Morien's friends hinted that I lacked the qualities he would need in a wife. Could I cook? The answer was no. Besides, I must have acquired some fancy ideas in Oxford: I would never be able to settle down for the long haul. On the other side, my Norfolk mentors regretted that they'd be losing my services and were concerned – were convinced – that I wouldn't be happy. In Wales he was harder to find fault with: he had a secure job, he had principles, he had earned golden opinions from a wide variety of people. He had no obvious vices other than smoking, and as for his intentions: from the word go he had not been merely committed to the idea that this was for keeps: he was hell-bent on it. And there was one other thing: he was clearly under the delusion that I was beautiful, and became irritated when I cast doubts on it. He believed it with such conviction that he almost made me believe it too. It was something like Eliza Doolittle's comment about being a lady – if somebody treats you as if you are, it becomes to all intents and purposes the truth.

A year later we were married. I borrowed a wedding dress because there was a war on and you couldn't get the coupons. Lots of neighbours rallied round, contributing precious donations of rationed sugar and butter towards the spread that was laid out in the vestry of Carmel chapel. There were two wedding cakes, because one of Morien's friends and comrades was in the bakery trade and so was my uncle Percy, and there'd been a lack of communication. The officiating clergyman was Morien's brother-in-law, Jack, a Baptist minister.

A few eyebrows were raised about that arrangement, including those of John Hampden Jackson in the last days before I said farewell to Norfolk. Why were we submitting to this farce when neither of us believed in it? Wasn't that hypocritical? Why not a simple private registry office without telling anybody, since marriage is the business of nobody except the two people concerned? I couldn't agree. In a properly functioning community it changes your relationship to everybody, not just to one person, and they had a right to be in on it if they wanted to. And they did want to. It wasn't quite what either side would have chosen, but they had bowed to it, and this was the only fun they were going to get out of it. As for Jack, he knew exactly what we believed and didn't believe. In his view we were good people and God wouldn't raise any objections to our being married in his chapel, so we responded in kind and didn't make a song and dance about it either. (And fifteen years later we were glad about that.).

CHAPTER 8

Wife and Mother

Morien took a job in Burnley Grammar School. Why Burnley? He wanted to be far enough from South Wales and Norfolk to ensure that nobody from our previous existence would keep dropping in to tell us how the process of living together should be conducted. The idea was to start from scratch and do it our way.

In some ways it was an auspicious time to start on a new life. Less than a month after the wedding came VE Day – the end of the war in Europe. The air raid sirens sounded the last all clear, and there was dancing in the streets. Elections were held and a landslide victory swept a new Labour Government with plans to build a brave new Britain. On the down side, the country was flat on its back having thrown everything it had into the war effort. The nation was so deep in hock that food rationing, far from being eased, continued to grow tighter during the first post-war years until at one stage even bread was rationed. Some voluntary aid came from America in the form of 'Bundles for Britain'. I remember having my first taste of tinned clam chowder.

Our immediate problem was finding somewhere to live, because so much had been destroyed by bombing, or fallen into disrepair. The government made what sounded like a madly Utopian promise to build a million new homes. In the end it kept that promise, but in April 1945 the first bricks still had to be laid, and we had no money for a deposit on any houses that did exist. So we spent the first months "in apartments" – two furnished rooms in somebody else's house. This was where I began to practice the trade that occupied the working lives of half the population: that of housewife. I had a lot to learn. Of course I'd seen it done, but only in the way that Morien had seen it done, without paying much attention. There was an assumption that these skills come naturally to any human being with xy chromosomes – but that is a myth, like the myth that all people with Welsh blood in them can sing.

One of the first skills I had to acquire was lighting the fire in the morning. Simple? You've got matches, haven't you? Okay, so you put some screwed-up paper under some sticks, but it goes out long before the sticks are alight, let alone the lumps of coal you're supposed to balance on top of them. That can keep on happening several times in a row. Being Billy's daughter, I put my faith in the system of trial and error. I learned to hold a newspaper in front of the grate to "make it draw" – and after the first time, how to do it without setting the paper on fire. I learned many things, for example that it's a mistake to make custard by putting custard powder into a glass jug (a wedding present) and adding boiling milk – it cracks the glass and makes a horrible sticky mess of your landlady's stove. I learned that if you wash woollens in hot water they are liable to shrink and you have to squander precious clothing coupons on replacing them. I learned that you can't make an omelette with dried egg, though you can make cakes with it. (The ration of eggs with shells on was one per person per week – but only if it was a good week.)

Tinned pilchards in tomato sauce figured largely on my menus, because a tin of them only took two points off the week's rations whereas a tin of corned beef could wipe off twelve points. One local source of animal protein was tripe, made of a sheep's stomach. This form of offal had long been a Lancashire delicacy, and even in those hard-pressed times it was unrationed and in plentiful supply because the rest of the country took the view that Lancashire was welcome to it. My mother had known how to make it very palatable and by trial and error I resurrected the art. It took some patience and a lot of onions. I even went to Burnley library to search for helpful hints about my new craft. There was one old-fashioned Mrs. Beeton-type book on home management. It told me among other things how to wash clothes by gently agitating them in soapy water, and declared that if the results were not satisfactory, I must have been guilty of "insufficient agitation."

That phrase has stuck in my mind because it seems to describe one of my character defects. Like Jimmy Porter in "Look Back in Anger", Morien was occasionally ruffled to find himself living with a "Mrs. Placid." I remember an occasion some years later when he told me we'd been burgled. I said "Oh." He thought I was seriously under-reacting. I'd like to say in my own defence that if anyone is in pain or in danger I get just as agitated as anybody else, but after all nobody'd been hurt – it was only stuff that had gone. I've noticed that many people find it seriously un-endearing if you say "Oh" when all around you are saying "Oh my gawd!!!" When that happens I remember the phrase "insufficient agitation" and try to remember to flap around a bit.

Long queues persisted at the Housing Office, but then came a breakthrough. We were offered accommodation, unfurnished, in a house in Prestwich Street. It hadn't been snapped up because it was only half a house – two old ladies were already living in the other half. We jumped at it, though. At last we could begin to play house in earnest, and acquire some furniture. We started out with a bed, table, four chairs, and a couple of tea chests supplied gratis by the nearest grocer.

Does it sound bleak? It felt more like a camping holiday. We were free and happy and independent. Morien had a bicycle, and I acquired a second-hand one to go with it, so that we could explore our surroundings. There was a cycling club with a large following in Lancashire, which gave access to rural retreats deep in the countryside around Burnley, run like youth hostels. Singles, couples, or families with children, could book in for a weekend in a beauty spot, enjoying fresh air and plain living, plus – if they had a taste for it – a spot of high thinking thrown in. There were always copies of Victor Gollancz's Left Book Club publications available on the bookshelves.

From this point in time it all sounds excruciatingly antique and quaint – sandals and rucksacks and earnest discussions and falderee, faldera. It felt good, though. After the end of the first term, we put the two bikes into the guard's van of a train heading north and cycled around Scotland, calling on another International Brigader and his wife, and taking in Loch Ness. I remember keeping a weather eye on the water just in case a small head on a long neck might put in an appearance, and I remember the name of the place where we stopped for refreshments. It was, predictably enough, the Ness Café.

I was pregnant. And I was thrilled. We'd taken no precautions to prevent this, but Morien's first reaction was a kind of astonishment. Sure, it was the kind of thing that ultimately happened to people, but to us? And so soon? When it was so nice the way things were, with just the two of us? I think it was Alex Comfort who defined marriage as a duel of two producers: it is rare for them to have exactly the same vision of how the final performance is going to turn out. To Morien this was a departure from the story line he had anticipated. To me it was one of the central themes.

Luckily at that point our half-a-house became a whole house, when the old ladies found other accommodation. As every monthly cheque came in we added touches of refinement to the ménage, such as curtains, a wardrobe, a sideboard, and now a cot and a large second-hand coach-built pram – a snip at four pounds. One notable thing about Britain under the new government was its solicitude for mothers and babies. As soon as the doctor confirmed you were pregnant, you became the privileged owner of a *green* ration book. That entitled you to go to the head of any food queue, instead of standing and shuffling for thirty minutes or so, and also entitled you to free milk, free orange juice and cod liver oil, and free check-ups and advice at the nearest clinic. That year's crop of babies, despite the shortages and the rationing, was by a wide margin the healthiest the nation had ever produced.

As an only child I hadn't absorbed much of the folk wisdom about baby-care, and some that I did remember seemed best forgotten. For example in the twenties an essential part of every baby's outfit was a "binder" – a strip of material to wind tightly round its tummy for three weeks to prevent it from growing up with its navel sticking out instead of neatly tucked in. In the valleys, prams were expensive and rare and push-chairs hadn't been invented, so babies were carried "Welsh-fashion." You asked somebody to hold the end of a long shawl, then backed off, wound the other end round the baby, then raised your right arm in the air and twirled around in the direction of the end-holder, winding the shawl round the baby and yourself and your left arm, and tucked the end in. The infant was thus held safely in place for the next few hours, leaving you with one arm free to do chores and shopping, and with no need of muscular exertion by the left arm. Babies held like that never seemed to cry. Little girls used to practice it on one another with their dolls, as automatically as they learned to tie shoelaces. All that knowledge had become obsolete while I was growing up.

The ETA for the new baby came and went. People started asking "You still here then?" because in those days it was legally laid down that for a first child you had to go into hospital. Finally labour pains commenced. I entered hospital, but then they subsided and didn't restart. I felt like a bed-blocker, but they couldn't send me home because the process had gone far enough to ensure that I couldn't pee without a catheter. Then the waters broke, but still nothing else happened. I cooked up a theory: it might be my old failing, of insufficient agitation. Perhaps when the pains come you're supposed to wonder: "What the hell's going on here?" and feel a stab of panic that floods the system with hormones and sets the whole process in operation? And all I'd thought was: "Oh good. And about time, too." Finally the medicos lost patience. A doctor approached with a syringe of inductive fluid and told me to turn over.

It was a fine boy. The doctor, having noted my Welsh accent, smacked him on the bottom and predicted that one day he'd play scrum half for Wales. The nurses voiced the equivalent of Dorothy Parker's wisecrack: "Congratulations – we knew you had it in you!"

The effect on Morien was surprising and instantaneous. He'd contemplated a theoretical baby without much enthusiasm, but this real live one looking back at him was a totally different matter. He couldn't wait to get home from school every day to learn what new thing Dylan had done or uttered or shown signs of responding to. I thought it must be the same thing that made him such a good teacher, but greatly enhanced. In a twelve-year-old boy you can see sometimes – maybe three or four times a term – the kick he gets out of understanding something he never understood before, and that is very rewarding to witness. But a baby's brain is growing much faster and making new connections every waking hour. It's fascinating to watch.

The rule then was that firstborns and their mothers stayed in hospital for two weeks, to be schooled in the conventional wisdom about child rearing. The regime was disciplinarian. It was not quite as stern as it had been in the twenties when experts like J. B. Watson warned mothers against playing with their babies. "Never hug and kiss them. Never let them sit on your lap", he wrote. "If you must, kiss them once on the forehead when they say goodnight. Shake hands with them in the morning." I can't believe mothers really behaved like that, except those who after shaking hands and saying "How do you do?" to their little darlings promptly handed them over to the nannies who really brought them up. Further down the social scale of course mothers had never sought instruction but had gone their own sweet way.

In the forties those doctrines were not entirely dead. Agony aunts in the magazines still warned against "smother-love." The guru Truby King advocated feeding the baby by the clock – and never a minute sooner just because it was yelling its head off. In hospital the babies were taken away and kept in a far-away room until it was time for them to be fed. The one thing they got right by today's standards was encouraging breast-feeding. I enjoyed doing that, echoing the sentiments of one young woman's father: "After you've been carrying those things around with you all these years, it must be nice to know that they actually work."

By the end of the two weeks in hospital, Dylan had become adapted to feeding at regular times, and sleeping through the night, and that does make things easier for parents. He was a very contented baby. The clinics were strongly opposed to the use of "comforters" – there was a rumour that sucking a dummy would distort the shape of a baby's mouth – but Dylan was quite unaffected by this ban. He was born already firmly addicted to sucking not his thumb, but the third and fourth fingers of his left hand – and nobody could remove those from the cot to cure him of the habit.

I thought of myself rather smugly as a very good mother, contrary to the prevalent belief that academics were absent-minded types and not to be trusted with responsibility for very young children. But one vivid memory raises a question mark over this. One day I emerged from a greengrocer's shop and walked half-way home deep in thought before panicking at the recollection that this was 1946 and I was a wife and mother and had left my baby parked in his pram on the pavement in the high street. I raced all the way back like the wind. Nobody had noticed. They'd assumed the pram's owner was in the shop. I can't remember what I'd been thinking about. Hardly, I think, about the meaning of life or any other of the great abstractions. It's more likely that I was wondering how to make the rations stretch to the end of the week.

Then one chilly morning in autumn, I woke and found that Dylan had somehow managed to kick off the blanket that covered him. I didn't know he was capable of that – it had never happened before. He wasn't crying but he was sucking his fingers very hard and his legs were cold. He caught a chill, and it went to his lungs, and the doctor came and shook his head and said he was seriously ill and there was nothing to be done except keep him warm and hope for the best.

The world came to a halt.

I lit a fire in the bedroom and did virtually nothing for the next three days but build up the fire and hold him and feed him and watch him while he slept and concentrate fiercely on willing him to get better... And he did get better. I had no God to pray to or to praise, but you can experience great waves of thankfulness without there being anybody on the receiving end. Morien had suffered too, and one way he reacted was by strengthening his determination that he would give no further hostages to fortune: one child was enough.

That was the only serious rift in the lute. After a couple of years I really wanted another child but Morien didn't. By that time – still many years before the pill – the fashionable mode of birth control was the rhythm method, as practised by Roman Catholics. David Lodge wrote a very funny novel about how that worked out in practice. It needed a lot of record keeping and joint determination to be alert for the slightest deviation from the cyclical norm and to stay always on the safe side. I can't pretend my heart was in it.

Our second son Gareth was born in 1949. It was still nearly twenty years before Dr. Spock transformed the nursery world by his book "Baby and Child Care" urging mothers to trust their instincts and not be dictated to by the experts. But I'd already arrived at a number of Spockish conclusions. Besides, Gareth was delivered at home by a midwife, and that made quite a difference. In hospitals you can keep babies far away from their mothers and let them yell till the clock says feeding time. You can't do that in the average house with a man who needs a decent night's sleep and neighbours who complain of the noise. Gareth got fed more or less on demand.

So there we were: a family, mum and dad and two children. In today's jargon I'd say it was certainly a functional family – mutually supportive, solvent, lubricated by plenty of love and give-and-take. Then around that time Dylan developed symptoms of asthma, and the doctor said that Burnley's climate and situation, while ideal for the cotton industry, was bad for respiratory diseases. Morien took instant action. He threw up his job, and we upped stakes and moved south.

CHAPTER 9

Idyll

On quitting Burnley, Morien's first job application – for the post of French master at Abertillery grammar school – was successful. It seemed a good omen. But achieving the next objective, an affordable roof over our heads, was a far more difficult problem. We had no money for a deposit on a house of our own, as newcomers we were right at the end of the queue for rented property, and there was no hope of temporarily sharing someone else's house as we had done when first married. The unspoken "no children" rule seemed as cast-iron as racist bans like "No blacks" or "No Irish" had ever been. When term started, Morien found lodgings for himself near the school, and I stayed with my mother while he spent his evenings exploring Abertillery and its hinterland on his motorbike, going ever further afield in his search.

One newspaper advert that had caught his eye had been placed by a rabbit-catcher. He turned out to be a rather posh rabbit-catcher, who had seen better days and been at one time a Formula One racing driver. Having fallen on hard times, the only saleable skill he possessed and was willing to exploit was a talent for killing things. Rabbits were a pest to farmers, and they would pay good money to have them eliminated from their land. That job meant that he was out for most of every day, but since his wife had recently walked out and left him high and dry, he urgently needed someone to run his house and look after the lifestock – dog, ferrets, and chickens – and put food on the table when he got back home, without expecting much in the way of wages.

He hadn't contemplated having two children also in residence, plus a husband at weekends (Abertillery was too far away for daily commuting). However, I was the only applicant, and asking no wages at all, so a deal was struck. My skill at skinning rabbits and making rabbit pie escalated over time into the realms of high art, and living rent free meant we could make a start on saving up for a deposit on a house. The arrangement lasted for a year.

At the end of that time we moved into a solid stone house with stunning views, standing in its own grounds. It was vacant, and was available rent-free to anyone who chose to live in it. It had nevertheless been empty for four years. It was a farmhouse built high on a mountainside a few miles from the village of Michaelchurch Eskley, near the border between Radnorshire and Herefordshire. There was no electricity, no gas, no telephone, no piped water, and no mains drainage. There was a lane leading up to the house but it led no further: that was the end of the line. There was no other human habitation within sight, but far away on the opposite side of the valley you could see smoke rising from the chimneys of our nearest neighbour. The nearest bus stop – to Hereford – was three miles away, and the bus only went twice a week. The house was called The Birches. The farmer who owned it simply wanted someone to move into it and keep it warm, because uninhabited houses soon deteriorate and when his eldest son married he would expect to live there. We took our furniture out of store and moved in, and there we spent a very rural twelve months.

During term time Morien continued to lodge in Abertillery, coming home up the mountain on his motorbike at weekends. Of course, I was only playing at being a countrywoman. As with most of the townies that move into Wales's rural areas, our lifestyle was subsidised. Once a week a van from the nearest village toured the outlying farmhouses bringing basic necessities like flour and coffee and soap and baked beans, and taking away a list of requirements for the following week, paid for in our case by money earned in town.

The realities of life on a hill farm are grimmer if you have to live off the land as well as living on it. We didn't have to plant and plough and hoe and shear and worry about the weather and the vet's bills and the harvest and the fat stock prices. Free of these burdens I could play at living the simple life and enjoy the idyllic side of it – the home baked

Dylan – number 1 son

Elaine at 19 years

Drummond – poet I knew
from university

Billy and Olive – parents

Gran and Gramp – grandparents

Gareth – number 2 son

Elaine at 11 years

Morien with Dylan
and Gareth

Morien Huw –
number 3 son

bread, the new laid eggs, the fresh milk. And there was the landscape – the foamy hawthorn blossom and the golden gorse and the lark in the clear air and the sunsets: "Yet shall your ragged moor receive the incomparable pomp of eve" and all that jazz.

Adjustments had to be made. We had to invest immediately in oil lamps: an Aladdin for indoors and a Tilley for going outside in the dark. Water came from a stream flowing past the house: you could fill the kettle from the stream. But within the first few weeks Morien installed a large tank in the dairy equipped with a tap, and filled it to the brim every weekend. The lavatory was at the end of the garden under a plum tree. There was a wooden seat, and underneath it a steep drop. There were no arrangements for the removal of night soil. So Morien redirected the course of the stream to flow underneath the steep drop and away down the mountainside as seemed to have been originally intended. It was fine in the daylight, and in the spring with the petals of the plum tree drifting down, but on a winter's night accompanying a small boy down the wet slippery path by the light of an oil lamp was not so much fun.

Everything took longer than it does in town. All the hot water for dishes, bathing and laundry, had to be boiled in a bucket over the little grate. The mountain mists got into everything. Before dressing the boys in the morning, I would light the fire and hold each garment in front of it till it stopped steaming, before putting it on. It sounds arduous, but it felt adventurous. For the first week, I really did feel cut off from civilisation, but the purchase of a second-hand battery powered wireless set reconnected me with the outside world. There was Radio Four, with the news and the discussions and the afternoon play and the comedians, and it felt like the last word in modern technology.

At first, milk was a problem because the cattle in those parts were raised for beef, and Morien would arrive at the weekend with sixteen bottles of sterilised milk on the back of his bike. Later we bought a goat – a British Saanen – and we called her Flake and I learned to milk her by trial and error.

It was a great place to bring up children in. They were free to wander at will. There was no traffic outside, and sometimes there were wild ponies. There were no visitors to drop in unexpectedly and wonder why the place was untidy. Children can drive you round the bend if there are other things that have to be attended to at fixed times, or if its crying offends the people in the flat upstairs. Gareth was very young – not yet potty-trained when we moved in – but if he kept me awake in the night it was no problem. When he finally dropped off, I dropped off too. Nobody was watching the clock.

And there was always something to do. We grew our own potatoes and gathered the rural freebies like blackberries, whinberries, hazelnuts, boletuses (woodland mushrooms) and watercress. People sometimes ask whether I wasn't bored. But think how long Jane Goodall spent alone in the jungle observing chimpanzees, and the last thing people ask her is: "Didn't you get bored?" I had a pair of young primates of my own to observe at close quarters, and found them fascinating.

For working farmers' wives the life was much harder. Some of them ran their own little marketable sidelines – raising ducks or making cheese – to ensure getting at least a little hard cash into their own pockets. A wife was as indispensable to a hill farmer as his horse, and not nearly as easy to find. So news of a young farmer's forthcoming marriage would be greeted by a buzz of excitement and envy: "Where did he get hold of her, then?"

For several months, I thought we were living at an outpost at the end of the inhabited world. But there were people living still further in the outback, with lifestyles reaching even further back in time. We exchanged visits with one couple who had heard rumours that the Birches was now inhabited, and invited us over, leading two staid horses for us to ride, each with one child in front, since it was too far for a child to walk. Neither of us had sat on a horse before, but both animals were being led and plodded along sedately. The farmhouse we arrived at had a huge open fireplace with one end of a felled tree blazing merrily under the chimney. The rest of the log reached far out into the room and was just ignored and stepped over, and when the lit end almost burned away to ash, someone lifted the end of the log and pushed it further in. That practice was probably as old as the hills. It saved all the trouble of sawing it up.

They had a mentally retarded son of about twelve who, if they'd lived in town, might well have been taken away and put into an institution. When he showed signs of agitated behaviour, his mother simply sat down and took him onto her lap and wrapped her strong arms tightly around him until he calmed down. I met her only once more. She came to the Birches alone on horseback, bringing a Toni Home Perm kit which she'd been given the year before as a present, but hadn't had the confidence to try to use on her own. We spent an interesting afternoon, memorable for cups of tea and girl talk and the powerful smell of ammonia. Then she rode away, curly-headed and happy, and I never saw her again.

Meanwhile, what about "Things of the Mind"? Well, once a fortnight the mobile library van came round the farms and you could borrow four books at a time. (The woman who drove the van said she had previously been a "shepherdess." But don't think of Dresden shepherdesses – it just meant she had professionally raised sheep.) She would bring a selection of books to tempt anybody who didn't know what they wanted to read, and if you did know what you wanted, she would get it for you. Also, every weekend Morien would bring home reading matter including a weekly copy of the New Statesman and the previous Sunday's Observer. I began sending in entries to the competition at the back of the New Statesman where you were asked to write something witty about a prescribed topic, sometimes in prose and sometimes in verse. I began trying my hand at that and sent in something every week under the initials E. M.

"Sent in" – how? The nearest postbox was a long way off. It wouldn't have been desirable to drag the kids there every week, especially in bad weather. But I persuaded all my kith and kin to send me letters often, even if they said nothing except: "Hi. How are you doing?" – because then the postman would call. Apart from the radio he was my chief contact with the outside world and told me all the local news, and he would take letters away as well as bringing them. I believe that technically it was against the rules for him to collect letters other than from a post box, but they were townies' rules and were among numerous regulations country people silently disregarded because they didn't make sense.

I began winning those NS competitions quite frequently, more regularly in fact than anyone else except a guy called Stanley J. Sharpless. I had to stop using the initials though. The New Statesmen sent me a polite letter saying that Sir Edward Marsh, a prestigious and influential figure in the literary world, had used those initials years earlier when he was a frequent contributor, and was now getting bothered by people commenting on his latest entries. He requested that this bogus E. M., whoever he might be, should stop impersonating him. So I threw off the mask and began signing Elaine Morgan. My name in print! And getting paid for it!! So all that education hadn't been entirely wasted after all.

I'm beginning to fear this account sounds too bland to be true, like the pastorals and eclogues of classical poetry with happy shepherds piping to their flocks. I'd better fill in some of the grittier bits or you won't believe it happened at all. One disquieting episode took place not long after we'd settled in. To light the Aladdin lamp you had to warm it first by igniting a clip soaked in methylated spirits. One evening I'd put out the flame on the clip and set it down on the table and didn't notice when Gareth toddled over and grabbed it. He burned his hand between the thumb and forefinger where it was hard to bandage, and over the next few days it showed no sign of healing but got more and more inflamed. No phone. No doctor's surgery for miles and no way of getting there. At the weekend Morien took Gareth down to the village on the motorbike, and returned with a supply of aureomycetin, and all was well – but it had been a bad few days.

I had to learn too about livestock. The farmer was disturbed when we bought the goat. Goats, he said, eat the bark off the fruit trees if they are not tethered and if they eat too much of it the tree dies. I promised to guard against that. But the fact was that Flake was a pedigreed lady, well fed and with fastidious tastes. She wouldn't have been seen dead eating the bark off a tree. We also acquired a dog without asking anyone's permission, and when lambing time came round it was shot without asking our permission. We never knew who did it.

Dylan was then of an age to start school. The nearest school was too far away for him to walk there but a school taxi, driven by the headmaster's husband, did the rounds collecting children from outlying farms, taking them to school and bringing them back. The Birches was more outlying than most but there was a picking-up point on his circuit about half a mile down the lane. On one occasion Dylan went to school and it rained all day and the taxi couldn't bring him back because of a bridge that was underwater and of course I had no way of knowing that he was marooned on the other side of the valley. Mrs. Williams at the Quakers farm brought him home by the short cut. It involved crossing a flooded footbridge knee deep in water, carrying Dylan in one arm and holding on to the handrail of the bridge with the other. It was kind and brave and I was very grateful.

While I was living at the Birches, I received an invitation to my mother's wedding. By that time she had been ten years a widow, her parents had both died, and she had settled down to a routine that suited her. She was on the list at the Pontypridd police station as an ideal person to take in and look after new recruits from outside the area. They were all young and nearly always male, and they appreciated being well fed and mothered. It was a job she did well and enjoyed doing, and she was well content. But there was a miner living in Jenkin Street whose wife had recently died. He was not young but was still working, and hated coming home to a cold and empty house. He began dropping in on Olive on various pretexts, staying for a cup of tea, doing useful little jobs around the house.

Finally, he put the proposition that instead of keeping house for a succession of strangers, she might consider doing it for one man who would always be there till death did them part. Each owned a house. If they married they could sell one and have a bit of money behind them. He was clearly a good man and very fond of her.

She very much wanted me to be at the wedding, to perform the equivalent of giving her away. This was pre-Flake, or I can't imagine how I would have managed it. Somebody would have had to milk that animal, and even in more populous places it's never easy to find a goat-sitter at short notice. As it was, I made the tortuous journey down the hill to the bus stop, bus to Hereford, train to Cardiff, change trains for

Pontypridd, bus to Hopkinstown, accompanied by a small boy, a child in arms, a boisterous young dog on a lead, and overnight luggage for the three of us.

Some weeks later, she wrote to report, with amazement, that Fred would get up early and before going to work in the morning would clean the grate and light the fire and lay the table for her breakfast, and beside her plate the newspaper would be folded to the page of the crossword she liked to do at that time of day. Many people in her life had treated her with love and gratitude for the way she cosseted them, but nobody had ever cosseted her before. She sounded as if she could learn to like it.

So that was life in the Birches. Then, after twelve months almost to the day, suddenly it was over. Morien heard that his old post in Pontypridd Grammar School had become vacant again. He applied for it and was appointed without the need of an interview. They knew his track record and were delighted to get him back. He found a fairly new bungalow in Aberdare, offered for sale at an affordable price partly because of its situation, behind the Abernant coal tips. Also, it had an adjacent paddock for the goat and the chickens. After two very frugal years we had saved enough to stop being rolling stones, and start gathering a bit of moss.

CHAPTER 10

Abernant

I had not expected our way of life to change so totally and so quickly. It was terrific, of course, to be able to walk into a room and switch the light on, and have hot water coming out of a tap, and a bathroom. The boys were entranced by these things. But I imagined we'd have the best of both worlds. We'd still have free milk and eggs. We had the paddock and a couple of outbuildings and open country behind us. We planned to install Dutch lights for growing vegetables under glass, and plant some fruit trees and raspberry bushes. But three incidents in rapid succession followed our arrival, so that in two weeks the pattern and direction of my life had radically altered.

First, Flake died. It happened so quickly and quietly that there was no time to call a vet. I don't know what went wrong. Maybe it was the trauma of the move, which involved a long journey in cramped conditions in the furniture van. Wild goats are as tough as old boots, but the pedigree ones can be more fragile and temperamental. That was a bit upsetting.

A few days later a fox killed all the six chickens, just for the hell of it because it couldn't have eaten or carried off more than one. How could that happen? Hadn't I locked them in for the night? No, because in the Birches that problem had never arisen. When the sun went down the fowls just put themselves to bed and were unmolested. If there were any foxes around they must have confined their ranges to the lusher lowland areas, following the strategy of the warriors of Dinas Vawr: "The mountain sheep are sweeter but the valley sheep are fatter. We therefore deemed it meeter to carry off the latter."

The third event was more exciting. Early one morning a telegram arrived. It came while we were still sleeping off our labours – moving house is a notoriously exhausting process – so I clambered back into bed to open it and read it aloud to Morien. Telegrams, for good or ill, were a big deal in those days, and this one was such a big deal that there were three pages of it.

Just before the move I had posted – from Michaelchurch Eskley via the postman, but giving the prospective new Abernant address – an entry for an essay competition being run by the Sunday Observer. The telegram announced that I had won third prize. Several Aberdare inhabitants who read the results in their Sunday newspaper were deeply puzzled when they read about this alleged Mrs. Morgan living in Little Row: they knew there was no such person.

The prize was £50 – a lot of money – but worth far more in terms of éclat and consequences. Three or four literary agents wrote around to the three winners offering to represent them if they were interested in turning professional. They all assumed that if we could write well enough to satisfy the Observer, we might have undiscovered first novels stashed away modestly in a drawer. I replied to one of them saying sorry, no novel, but turning professional sounded very interesting and how does one go about it? The answer was unequivocal, especially in the case of a female writer. The insatiable market in those was for romantic short stories for women's magazines.

Over the next couple of years I sold maybe half a dozen. The agent would send them first to Woman or Woman's Own and then re-submit to less and less lucrative outlets and maybe end up with a small cheque from My Weekly of Dublin. But I didn't have the rejection letters coming through my post box which would have been terminally discouraging, and the occasional acceptance qualified me in my own mind as one of the numerous people up and down the country who are "trying to be" or "supposed to be" writers.

The bungalow was called "Noddfa" – Welsh for "refuge." It had been recently built, but it was adjacent to half a dozen smaller and much older houses. These houses had once been famous for their stunning display of roses, richly fertilised by manure from the pit ponies. Since then, two coal tips between Little Row and the rest of Abernant had grown higher and higher. Little Row had long been out of sight of the rest of the community, and in one important respect out of mind, too, in that there was no refuse collection. Rubbish was simply dumped at the bottom of one of the tips, just across the lane from Noddfa, where it provided a living for a thriving colony of rats.

Morien visited the council offices, reported the situation as a health hazard, and requested action. He was told nothing could be done because the only access to the houses, the unmade lane between the tips, was traversable by a motorcar or a small van, but not by the council's refuse trucks. Morien came home and thought again. He paid another visit to the council offices with a statement of intent. He planned, he said, to buy a couple of refuse bins, fill them up, notify the local newspaper and its photographer of his intention, and then empty them onto the steps of the Town Hall, together with a dozen or so dead rats, simply to draw attention to the problem.

It was then the council's turn to think again. They discovered that they did in fact have a smaller vehicle that had been unaccountably overlooked but would serve the purpose. Nobody was more surprised than the inhabitants of Little Row, who tacitly promoted Morien to the position of their unpaid legal adviser and consultant on all aspects of social problems and public relations.

We continued nest-building. Morien laid a new cement path around the house and installed a damp course, while I did wallpapering and made curtains. Dylan attended one of the new Welsh schools, and Gareth joined him there when he was old enough.

One bit of excitement did flare up and then fizzle out. Getting bored with writing short-story variations on the theme of boy meets girl, I attempted to write a play intended for the theatre and aspiring to be a drawing-room comedy, since I'd been assured that was the most saleable genre at the time. When I sent it to my agent, he hawked it around the West End, where it prompted no encouraging noises except from Emlyn Williams. Emlyn declared (perhaps out of politeness or Celtic solidarity) that it had merit, but he was just going off to South Africa, so he could do nothing about it. It ended up, like the stories that ended up with My Weekly, in the last port of call. It was sent to an address in London where the BBC was exploring the possibility of creating a genre of drama suitable for televising. They bought it.

Television in those days was no kind of Mecca for serious dramatists. Established writers and successful actors would not look at it because the pay was derisory, production values were amateurish, the screens were small and grey and bleary, and the show was irrevocably doomed to close in a week: there could be no prospect of a long run however favourable the reception. It was unpopular even with hard-up actors. They had to learn a whole part to be played just once. Mishaps that would later be called "out-takes" went out live and were witnessed all over the country. If you forgot your lines you couldn't faff around for a few minutes until your fellow players guided you back on course because the play had to end at a prescribed time, to give way to the sacrosanct nine o'clock news. Any wasted screen time might have to be made up by gabbling through the heart-rending final scene at the speed of an express train. The medium was in the Keystone Cops stage of its history, except that there was not much comedy in its repertoire.

Naturally, then, material specially written for this medium was non-existent. The people in charge had experience of audiences at West End first nights, but they were often the kind of people who thought a tv set was something the servants liked to watch. Nobody knew what the actual viewers wanted to see. In this seller's market, then, they took my play. We had no tv set – very few people had them in those days – but we managed to find someone who did and was willing to let us watch it.

Frankly, it was pretty awful. Newspapers then devoted only a tenth as much space to reviewing tv as they did to reviewing live theatre. But one of the top critics, Philip Hope-Wallace, found room to pronounce it the silliest play the BBC had ever broadcast.

Goodbye to all that, then. Okay, I could live with that. Wife and mother, two lovely children, inexpensive little hobby scribbling the odd love story when you've got nothing better to do – who could ask for more? But when I looked forward I saw the time when the boys would

have grown up and left home and there'd be years and years ahead …
I was going to get very bored. I was going to suffer from empty nest
syndrome.

The idea grew on me. I told Morien I wanted another baby. But
what Morien wanted was a car. He thought once the boys were a bit
older I could get a job teaching – maybe in an infants' school. That
would certainly keep my mind occupied! We'd be a two-income family
and could afford to run a car and have holidays abroad. It would be
ideal. Another baby would ruin all that.

I put forward a wildly fanciful proposition. I wanted to be a writer,
not a teacher. If I could earn a thousand pounds without going out of
the house, that would prove I had earning power that wouldn't stop
dead at the birth of another child. I wouldn't spend any of it: I'd save it
up for us to buy a car with. I'd put it in a special account. (Was there a
subliminal memory of Olive's Vice Box?) If he would promise that we'd
go in for another baby when I'd achieved that, I would promise not to
nag or say another word about it until that time came…

He grinned. He couldn't believe his luck. After the fiasco of the tv
play, it sounded as if I was saying "If I should win the pools…" But we
shook hands on it. And from then on I was not just tinkering around
with the idea of becoming a writer. I was as motivated as hell. Could I
write a novel? It would take too long. Something academic? That
doesn't pay. Literary critic? It's what an Oxford English degree equips
you for, but you'd have to move in the right circles and know the right
people. Not a dog's chance. Radio plays? I sold one of those to Radio
Wales. Talks for Woman's Hour? I sold two of those…

Around that time, the little enclave of BBC talent charged with
the task of feeding the cameras decided to become pro-active. They
offered a prize of ninety pounds for a ninety-minute play written for
television. The winner would be announced at the Cheltenham
Literary Festival and the winning play would be televised.

I was in with a chance. My earlier experience of the medium,
however disastrous, had given me a few clues about what works and
what doesn't. That might give me a slight edge on those competitors
(probably 100%) who had no experience of it at all. I wrote a play in

which Oscar Wilde on his visit to the United States got stranded overnight, due to some mishap to the wheel of a carriage, among some hillbilly characters. I figured that the cinema-going viewers would have seen enough cowboy films to be comfortable with that setting, the judges could be kept happy with some Wildean epigrams, and the producer would be glad there was only one set and a very cheap one at that. There were over a thousand entries for that competition. And *Wilde West* was the winner.

I attended the Cheltenham Festival where the result was announced, and met some people from BBC television including the Head of the Script Department, Donald Wilson. He welcomed me aboard and drew up a contract by which I would undertake to write four more plays in the next twelve months. Those guys were seriously headhunting. Later they asked BBC Wales to organise an event open to anyone who had ever had any kind of writing published anywhere. They came down to Cardiff like recruiting sergeants, promising that this new medium was going to become HUGE. I'm sometimes asked how I managed to break into television script writing, but in the early fifties if you could write at all you didn't have to break in, you got sucked in. It was 75% luck, being in the right place at the right time.

Morien adjusted rapidly to the idea that I was no longer in the supposed-to-be-a-writer stage and was now a real one. If he was surprised, he disguised it very well. He decreed if this job was going to be done, it had better be done properly. We learned that the Cheltenham success had been jeopardised when one of the judges, John Fernald, took a batch of the entries to read in the sunshine on top of a cliff. A stiff breeze blew several pages of Wilde West out of his hand and he was exasperated on running around and collecting them, because they not only lacked staples but were not even numbered.

Such a thing must never happen again. Morien, from his teenage years, had acted as secretary to his father when Johnny was chairman of the lodge, and he once pretended to think I'd only married him for his typewriter. From that point on, I wrote plays in the messy longhand that I found much quicker, and he transformed them into flawless professional-looking artefacts. He sometimes put comments in the margins of the first drafts – "Didn't understand this" – "this scene is boring." That was invaluable. If he was baffled or bored the viewers would be too – so, back to the drawing board.

In those days – long before Television Centre – the BBC was short of studio space in London. They needed some programmes produced in the regions and fed into the network to give London a bit of breathing space before going back on air. So once every month a full-length one-off drama was produced in Cardiff by local writers, directors, producers, designers, and actors, and it went out live all over the country. The same happened in Scotland and Manchester. For the first time, English people became accustomed to plays in which people with regional accents appeared not only playing maids and comic policemen, but featuring as heroes and heroines.

The term "kitchen sink" is normally used to describe the series of exciting and long-running plays created on the West End stage by John Osborne, Arnold Wesker, Sheila Delaney and others, and the assumption is that they originated it. But their work had been preceded by television plays of that genre. I found it exhilarating to be a part of all that.

Meanwhile the special account was growing satisfactorily, giving good reason to hope that the £1,000 target would be reached before there was any need to start worrying about the ticking of the biological clock.

CHAPTER 11

Playwright

Between 1955 and 1960 I was fairly prolific by the standards of the time. I sold fourteen single plays and a four-part serial. A couple of the more popular ones were repeated – with different producers and casts since they were still going out live and not recorded. One of these was a murder play with a difference: nobody dies. A man who suspects his wife of infidelity arranges for her to be poisoned in his absence. He discovers he was mistaken and the suspense lay not in "Whodunnit?" but in "Can he undo it in time?" Then there was a nativity play and that was different too. Mary, the shepherds and the magi were not in the cast list. It was the day after Mary fled, and consisted of interactions between the wife of the innkeeper and one of the soldiers drafted in to slaughter the innocents.

Some were what would now be called drama-documentaries, on such topics as the eleven plus examinations, or social workers, or opencast coal mining. In those days any item on tv had more impact because there was only one channel. If I got on a bus and overheard somebody saying:"Did you watch that thing on tv last night?" I would listen to what they said. It constituted a kind of opinion poll before the Beeb set up its Audience Research Unit. One indication of the growing influence of television was that when I met Ted Willis at a Writers' Guild meeting in 1958, he was feeling pleased because one of his "Dixon of Dock Green" episodes had been quoted in the House of Lords. And my opencast play, *Black Furrow*, had been quoted in the House of Commons.

But such visits to London were rare. The job mainly consisted of sitting down and writing a script, posting it, and later watching it at home. (After the first three we bought our own tv set.) Most of them were produced in Cardiff and I sometimes went down for a read-through or a rehearsal. Rehearsals were held in a hired hall with sticky-tape outlines on the floor to indicate where the doors and the furniture would be on the real set. I remember how the actress Jessie Evans laughed when the emotion she put into one speech brought tears to my eyes, even though I'd written it myself. But then, if you can't make yourself laugh or cry, how can you hope to do it to anybody else? Incidentally, that was the first script of mine to be blue-pencilled by the BBC. Donald Wilson ruled "You'll have to change that line. Nobody can say bugger on television." That shows how long ago it was.

Another indication of how long ago it was occurred in 1959 when Donald asked me to come to London to discuss future plans. He was urging me to write a serial about a girl from the valleys who wins a scholarship to Oxford, and to instruct me in the art of writing serials. In those days, the decision-makers at the BBC were not suits, with degrees in business management, but creative types with first hand experience of doing what they were asking other people to do. If scripts failed to come in fast enough, Donald was quite capable of knocking one out for himself.

When I arrived, he gave strict instructions to the secretary in the outer office that he was on no account to be disturbed, and was not available to take phone calls *until further notice*. I followed him in and sat down with an empty notebook and ball-pen at the ready, to take instruction. You start out, he said, with separate threads, and in the end they must all come together, like this. He drew a diagram. He also passed on a maxim well known in the trade. What makes good drama, he said, is when somebody is trying to do something and somebody else is trying to stop him. People to whom I've passed on this advice find it vague or simplistic, but very often, when I had a sick script, I found that formula more therapeutic than later buzzwords like "too linear" or "needs more jeopardy."

That entire seminar lasted about twelve minutes. Then he asked me if I liked tennis, pointed to a heap of magazines I could amuse myself with if I didn't, and settled down to watch Wimbledon, safe from anybody barging in to pester him with unnecessary questions. I don't know how the BBC top brass conducts itself these days, but I'd be surprised to learn that they are quite as laid back as that.

The serial he asked for was called "A Matter of Degree." It was in six episodes, and about midway through there was a crisis. During the last-but-one rehearsal, one of the actresses returned from a protracted visit to the Ladies looking chalky white. She'd had a miscarriage. She was a trouper, trained to believe that the Show Must Go On, but she wasn't sure she'd be up to it. The situation called for a swift re-write, and I wrote in some busy scenes for the other players to explain why she appeared in that episode only briefly, delivering her few remaining lines while reclining on a sofa. By the following week the actress, the character, and the story line were back on the rails, and people quite forgot to wonder what was the subtle dramatic significance behind her sudden indisposition.

The serial proved very popular. In the script one of the friends and relatives giving the heroine a send-off calls out: "Knock 'em cold, kid!" One of the neighbours in Pontypridd had been on the station and called that out to me as I got onto the train for Oxford for the very first time. It was also used as the headline of a full-page review in the London Welsh magazine. Around that time too, one national newspaper ran a light-hearted article about the need of new blood in the House of Lords, illustrated by the names and pictures of six characters that might improve the chamber's relevance to modern life. One was Spike Milligan and one was Elaine Morgan. That was a high spot. My standing within the trade as a bankable writer and adapter was sustained, but tv had now begun to attract high-class star actors and actresses and on-screen personalities, and viewers ceased to register who was writing the words.

Script-writing did very little to disturb the even tenor of life in "Noddfa". The boys were growing up and doing well. Dylan was in Aberdare Grammar School. Shortly before taking the eleven plus, he had fallen out of a tree and broken his arm and had to sit the exam with one arm in plaster, but he passed with flying colours all the same. Gareth, still in the Welsh school, was growing up with an absorbing interest in wild life. I remember one day when he came home carrying a snake, and handed it to me to hold while he checked the markings in a book he had, to find out whether it was poisonous or not. Morien taught them to play chess, and at a later date how to drive a car. In the summers we took a week's holiday on the Gower peninsula, first in a caravan and later in a boarding house.

Later there came a development that did threaten to rock the boat. BBC Wales, in common with other regions, experimented with putting on its own chat show, inviting well-known figures to their studio to be interviewed. The show was called "Crosstalk" and it went out every week. The plan was to have two hosts – in practice they turned out to be two hostesses – doing the interviewing in alternate weeks, and I was invited to be one of them. It sounded interesting and only involved one day a fortnight. So I took it on, interviewing characters like the Welsh millionaire Julian Hodge, and Lord Chalfont, and Gerald Navarro, the flamboyant Tory MP with the superabundant moustache.

Being in front of the camera is a totally different proposition from being behind it. A freelance writer can take a couple of weeks off at any time if the need arises, but if the Radio Times says you're going to appear you've got to be there, and on time. And you have to look right. I should have remembered the wise precept of Thoreau: "Beware of any enterprise that requires new clothes." Before Morien's very eyes I began to mutate into a quite different woman from the one he married. I took to fussing about my hair, dashing out to buy a new roll-on, anguishing whether I was getting a cold sore on my lip, and fretting: "That's no good, I've worn that three times already." Once every fortnight I was liable to be chucking my weight around, shucking off responsibility, breezing off saying "Don't ask me, it'll have to wait. I'm sorry, somebody else will have to cope with that."

The ironic thing was that, in those days at least, if anyone had seen the programme and mentioned it, nine times out of ten they never remembered a word of what I or anybody else had *said*. They were just mesmerised by the fact that anybody they knew in the flesh could be appearing on that little screen. One woman, I remember, commented on the fact that my hair had been "moving." She didn't mean it stirred her emotions. She'd been surprised, because at that date the hair of adult women was apt to remain motionless – as Margaret Thatcher's still did, much later. If this woman had seen me in the street in Aberdare with moving hair, she'd have thought: "What's the matter with her, for heaven's sake? Why can't she get around to having a proper perm, like everybody else?" But because it was on the telly, she thought: "Oh, so that's the way they have it now, is it?"

Frederick Raphael later wrote a book called "The Glittering Prizes," and part of it was set at around that date. One character was a man living quietly and happily with his wife and children in the country, on a shoestring. An old friend from his Cambridge days visits him and offers to help out by finding his wife a job. It's in television. Later there's a scene where the man sits alone at home, polishing the stock of his rifle and watching the screen. Raphael wrote: "The sound jarred, so he went and turned it down. Joyce appeared, mouthing intelligently, her head cocked on one side, in the manner sharp satirists were already imitating. After a time, he closed the gun with a practised snap of the wrist, took aim, and, without any change of expression, shot his wife." Now Morien was emphatically not a shootist, and he at no time asked me to stop doing the show. But I knew he was wondering where this new trajectory was likely to end up. After a few months I informed the BBC that my next appearance on Crosstalk would be my last. It was quite easy to do. There had been no contract, and it gave them a month to find a replacement.

To a later generation of feminists, that was the kind of thing that made them puke. They would point out that if the positions had been reversed the man's career would have come first and the family would have had to fit in, and they would be right.

It's true that if I had yearned for the bright lights it might have been unhealthy and pusillanimous to bottle up those ambitions, and it could well have poisoned the relationship. But that wasn't the way it was. The experience had been a nice little ego-trip. "Been there, done that, good to know I can do it if the need arises." But it really wasn't my metier. If it had been a question of giving up writing it would have been very different. If my talent had been for acting it would have been very different. But I personally didn't like the unfamiliar "get out of my way" sound of my own voice when the fortnightly date loomed, as if how I looked and what I said became vastly important as soon as the camera was pointed in my direction. That was rubbish.

Besides, in case you've forgotten, the whole writing-for-television venture had originally been a means to an end. That end was very close to being attained. The special fund had reached its target of £1000. The future that Morien had once envisaged had changed. It had become very unlikely that I would settle down to becoming a housewife pure and simple once the boys were grown up, or that I would become a teacher. Without a third child to occupy my attention, there seemed little doubt that I would become *something* or other, but it was not easy to predict what it would be.

So the terms of the pact were activated without demur. Morien found a friend to teach him how to drive, took the test and threw away the L-plates, and went out and bought himself a car. No nonsense about hire purchase agreements, just sign a cheque, and take to the road. And then come home and fulfil his side of the bargain.

CHAPTER 12

Quest

There followed a long period of frustration. On the fertility front, nothing happened. And kept on not happening. Unhappy women pining for a baby have often related how that feels. I have every sympathy for them, and cannot claim that kind of sympathy for myself because I already had two children and a career. I "had it all", and was just being greedy. No excuse for feeling that way. No getting rid of it, either.

I did at one point consult a doctor. In those days there was little or nothing you could do about it. He mentioned my age. Well, yes, that had occurred to me. He mentioned, without actually recommending, some stuff called Fertilol. I think it was some kind of snake oil or placebo. No good. I had to face the facts. "We could", I ventured, "adopt?" Well, I admit that was pushing it. That had never been mooted and was no part of the deal, but Morien agreed to go the extra mile and we started down that road. I have to tell you it's a longer road than it looks, and in this case was something of a race against time. While a woman can biologically conceive after the age of forty, that age is considered a watershed when it comes to adopting. They won't look at you. I was by then thirty-seven.

The first organisation we approached asked a lot of questions, seemed happy with the answers, and merely asked for a letter from our vicar, or the minister of our chapel. We didn't have a vicar, or a minister. I hadn't realised how much this branch of good works was driven by the desire to save the souls of these little children. I hadn't realised either how much competition there was. Back in the twenties, if you adopted a baby, you were doing a kind deed, saving it from an orphanage. But by the fifties, even though the pill hadn't been invented, there were already far fewer unwanted pregnancies. Babies for adoption had become an increasingly scarce resource, and people were queueing up for them.

We finally discovered an organisation that didn't bar agnostics – the Glamorgan County Council. We were visited and vetted by a succession of social workers to ensure that we were of good repute, and capable, and solvent, and so on, and that the boys as well as their parents were prepared for the advent of their little sister. Because yes! Adoption did have that one advantage over natural childbirth: you could express a preference for a boy or a girl. I chose "girl". I thought it might influence Morien's attitude to what women are made of, if he could get to know one of them from the ground up, as it were. It was worth a try anyway.

Eventually, the great day arrived when we received a letter about a beautiful little girl who could be collected in two week's time. I set about installing the necessary equipment and knitting pink. Then came shattering news. The baby girl had regrettably and unexpectedly died. I told myself over and over again how much worse it might have been. It could have happened a few days after we'd taken her home, instead of before we'd ever seen her. I'd have been tormented by feelings of guilt as well as bereavement, in case there had been some symptom I should have recognised, something I should have done differently. I tried to feel grateful for that, but it was hard. As for trying again – nah! The fight had finally gone out of me. It was all over.

Then I heard from Rose Hacker, a remarkable character I'd got to know through a correspondence club. She was a member of the London County Council and involved in a whole range of voluntary initiatives involving women and children. She happened to know of a schoolgirl of sixteen, planning to give up her baby for adoption. But it was a boy. Would I still be interested? I shot up to London like a greyhound out of the slips, taking with me an empty carrycot. And this time nothing went wrong. Rose came with me to the home to collect him. I was asked to change his nappy, to demonstrate how capably I could handle him. I was a veteran in that department and I passed with flying colours. They then asked me to mix his feed. Ah! That I'd never had to do, but the instructions were on the tin and I followed them to the letter. I took him home on the train. At the end of the statutory six-week period we were notified that his mother had signed the necessary confirmation that she had not had second thoughts, and the baby was ours.

It then only remained for the adoption to be made legal and binding by being ratified by a judge. The judge in question who had to perform this rite was known to take a keen interest in the spiritual welfare of children being adopted, and always included a question about it. I was on tenterhooks in case the Vicar question might even now put us back to square one. He bent his head over all the documents in front of him and after various other questions he said, "I see that you were married in the Baptist chapel in Hopkinstown." "Yes, your Honour." "And I take it that you intend to bring up the child to share your own beliefs?" "Oh yes, your Honour!" I have sometimes since had the unworthy thought that it cannot have been pure luck that he phrased it quite like that. Perhaps one of the social workers had a quiet word with him and convinced him that, as agnostics go, we were respectable and benevolent and clean living and had all the civic virtues except attending a place of worship.

We called him Morien Huw Morgan. The first time I took him to Aberdare a woman came up to me to commiserate on the assumed failure of our family planning arrangements – such bad luck that this had happened after an eleven-year gap, just when we had a right to expect that things were getting easier. I said no, I had wanted him. She smiled knowingly, and said "Well of course you've got to *say* that, haven't you?" It only took three words to convince her.

The new arrival turned out to be a sturdy baby with a wide grin, as merry as a cricket. Morien had a special protectiveness towards him, regarding him at some level as a waif that we had rescued, rather like the stray cat that moved in on us some years later. I never saw him as a waif in any respect. He was, as the old wives used to say, eminently "fit to live" and stand up for himself. I have never had the slightest cause to regret taking him on, and plenty of reasons to feel glad that I did.

There's a postscript to this. Fifty years later, a letter arrived saying that his birth mother, living in Essex, had spent the past two years trying to trace the name and whereabouts of the child she had given up for adoption, and enquiring whether he would be willing for her to be put in touch with him. They exchanged letters and photographs and e-mails. His mother Carol and I talked on the phone and later she came down for a visit. It has been a positive and fascinating experience all round. She came down to see us, Huw arranged to go up and meet his half-sister and three nephews and now has a whole raft of new relations. I almost feel as if I have too, though the relationship is not easy to define: "This is Carol, my son's mother" is always going to sound odd.

I feel chastened now to remember how little thought I gave, when I visited that home, to the young girl who was in fact at that moment upstairs looking out through the window and watching us go. I knew nothing about her and I wasn't the cause of her grief, but I should have been more aware that somebody somewhere must have been losing what I was gaining.

CHAPTER 13

Liberation Now

It took me some time to fall into the old baby-raising routine, but not too long. It's like having learned to ride a bike – you never really lose the hang of it. Besides, the world had moved on and it was getting a lot easier, with more mod cons – not only electric light and hot and cold running water, and the godsend of a fridge, but also an early model of a washing machine. In short, it was the time when technology was trying to transform the role of most housewives from a life of hard labour into the occupation of the radiant young woman beginning to appear in advertisements. She was portrayed as pert and chirpy, with high heels and trim ankles and a cute frill on her dinky little apron. She was never seen scrubbing the floor or cleaning the lavatory, but often flicking a feather duster, trying out a new recipe for butterfly cakes, and ecstatic on being told that Persil washes whiter. Not only for the advertisers, but for the economists too, productivity was thought of as overwhelmingly the role of males, subdivided into Capital and Labour. Women were not thought of as either Capital or Labour. Our economic role was obvious, even to J. K. Galbraith. It was to "facilitate consumption." In other words, we did the shopping.

But I was still involved in a different kind of production. My agent, Harvey Unna, had registered some impatience when told that I expected soon to have a baby to look after. He made the usual assumption that it must have been an "accident" (women are so careless). He regarded it as unprofessional, and was not wholly cheered to learn that it was a deliberate choice. (Women have a strange sense of priorities.). He wondered how many years it would be before I would send him another script. He needn't have worried. My output slowed down a bit but it never really dried up.

We invested in a play pen, and while the toddler was safely pottering about inside it, I could sometimes get some pages written, and some more after he was asleep. Morien circulated the anecdote that he had come home one day to find the roles reversed. I was seated inside the play pen, safe from interruption, and Huw was toddling around at large, emptying the book case and playing with the fire-irons. It made a good story but it never really happened.

During term time, in any hours I did have to myself, I acquired the knack of complete concentration on writing and becoming completely oblivious to my surroundings. Too completely, sometimes. On Sunday mornings, Morien would take Huw off in the car to visit his grandparents in Ynysybwl and give me a break. On one such occasion, a spark from the kitchen fire set light to a garment dangling from the airing rack. When it was well alight the remains of it fell onto a chair and the upholstery began smouldering. I was in the other room, and by the time I became aware of what was happening, the kitchen ceiling and walls, and everything contained in it, had been blackened with acrid smoke. It would all need redecorating. It felt a bit like the time when I'd walked home and left Dylan in his unattended pram.

In the seven years after adopting Huw, I sold one radio play, seven single television plays, and five serials, four-part or six-part, some of them adaptations. Life seemed to be ticking over quite happily. We made our last move, from Abernant to Mountain Ash, a few miles down the valley. From there, Morien had a shorter drive to the school in Pontypridd, but would still be far enough away from it to be able to go to the pub in the evening with no likelihood of bumping into any of his sixth-formers. He liked to keep home and work in separate compartments, and so did I.

Shortly after the move, something began to happen which would change my life quite dramatically. When I visited Mountain Ash library I would take out one novel, and a non-fiction book on the second ticket. One day I came home with Desmond Morris's best-selling book "The Naked Ape." It dealt with fascinating questions such as why humans are so different from apes, and whether the way we behave can be explained in terms of the experiences of our prehistoric ancestors. I found some more books on this theme, such as Robert Ardrey's "African Genesis" and "The Hunting Hypothesis."

They were all deeply interesting, informative, well argued, written to be accessible to the general reader, and claiming to be an account of the evolution of the human race. And yet the more I read of this genre, the more I found that the fascination was being modified, and in the end swamped, by a much stronger emotion – an explosive compound of scepticism and outrage. I felt this is all nonsense! These people are not thinking straight. They're not thinking or writing about the human race, only about the evolution of less than half of the human race – namely, adult males.

I was not qualified to question the science – I only had O-levels in the sciences. As for the relations between men and women, I had no personal experiences to embitter me. In my working life I was paid the rate for the job with no discrimination on grounds of sex. I had no first-hand experience of men being abusive, either to me personally or to any of my friends or relatives. The four people I lived with all happened to be males, but none the worse for that. What had got into me to make me indignant now?

Up to that point, whenever I'd thought about social inequality and injustice, I'd envisaged it on class lines, not on gender lines. I had of course read and been stirred by the history of the suffragettes and their fight for the right to vote. But like the campaign to abolish slavery, it seemed to be an episode from far-off days, a brave story with a happy ending, about a wrong that had been righted. We had the vote. The names that have come down to us from the first wave of protests, apart from that of Annie Kenny, are in the main the names of middle-class women. That was inevitable. But it did mean that many of the things they focussed on failed to resonate in the kind of community where I was brought up. Florence Nightingale complained bitterly of the maddening boredom and waste of women's lives, spent in endlessly dressing up, and paying calls on each other, and going out to dinner. Millions of women would have reacted: "I should be so lucky!" Unlike

Ibsen's heroine, they were not there for decoration, for the relaxation of the tired business man, and none of them lived in Doll's Houses.

I was to feel the same about some issues raised in the seventies. One grievance voiced was that all the "shitwork" in daily life was performed by women. Isolated in their separate houses, they mopped the floors and changed the nappies and cleaned the lavatories while their husbands worked in nice clean offices with secretaries to bring them cups of coffee. It had some truth in it but it was a class-conditioned attitude. Women whose husbands and sons worked underground were hardly in a position to voice that particular gripe. There aren't many jobs shittier than mining.

Looking back, I can only think of one occasion when I have felt personally victimised for being a woman. I arrived in Paddington Station one evening to stay overnight in order to attend a meeting at ten the next morning. I booked into a bed and breakfast nearby and went in search of a meal. I entered a restaurant and picked up a menu but a waiter asked me to leave. He had been forbidden to serve any unaccompanied female on the grounds, it transpired, that she might be a hooker looking for a likely customer. It seemed the height of injustice. And I was very hungry. I pointed to a solitary male – why had he not been ejected because he might be looking for a hooker? The waiter shrugged – he was only carrying out orders. It was the only time in my life when I have briefly felt that if there had been a rock handy I might have hurled it through the plate glass window. Instead I approached the nice middle-aged couple at the next table, who turned out to be Americans, and they were happy to invite me to sit down with them. While I was their guest, no one could lay a finger on me.

However, I'm sure that had nothing to do with my reaction to Desmond Morris's book. I simply and strongly felt that he'd got it wrong. The theme – which was the accepted wisdom among scientists for a major part of the twentieth century – was that people are different from apes because apes' ancestors stayed in the trees and our own ancestors went out onto the plain and became hunters. They stood up on two legs to run faster, they became naked because the running overheated them. They became more ferocious and bloodthirsty than the vegetarian apes, and fought one another to get access to scarce resources. Ardrey in particular identified aggression as the badge of all our tribe.

Not in females, of course. Females were regarded chiefly as one of the scarce resources for the males to fight over. If they differed from the males in any way, that was to make themselves more sexually attractive, because if they weren't sexually attractive why would any mighty hunter condescend to throw them an occasional lump of meat to keep them alive? This is of course a rough caricature of what the books actually said, but it was the message that was coming across to me, however much more elegantly they expressed it.

But why in heaven's name did the females of our species have to evolve special features to coax the males to desire them? In every other species known to man (or should I say known to humans?) the males take what they are offered in the way of pulchritude, and they like it. A male warthog thinks a female warthog is the most desirable thing he ever saw or smelt. Male gorillas show no signs of thinking "Hmph! Don't think much of that one. I think I'll leave her there and scout around for something a bit more willowy. Less hairy, perhaps. And two bigger bumps on her chest wouldn't come amiss." So just what entitled the ancestors of this one particular anthropoid to get so goddam picky?

That was in 1967, and there were a lot of other questions I wanted to ask. I felt sure that somebody qualified to pronounce on these matters would soon start asking them, and write a book about it, and I could read the book. I waited a couple of years, and then another couple of years, and then I got tired of waiting. I opened a brand new exercise book and wrote: "The Descent of Woman. Chapter One."

CHAPTER 14

Lift-off

I wrote it all down, more or less without pausing for breath, unpacking my heart of a lot of things I had been feeling and thinking. The first words were: "According to the book of Genesis, when God created Man, Woman was not merely an afterthought, but an amenity." It went on to say that the scientific narratives brought in to replace the myth of the Garden of Eden bore the same hallmarks of having been concocted by males, for males, and about males. As each chapter was completed, I handed it to Morien and he typed it out.

What did he have to say about it? It's a good question with an unexpected answer that you may find hard to believe. We never talked about it. It was just like typing out the plays. Occasional comments: "This part is not quite clear" ... "You're repeating yourself." It was a subject he had thought about. In fact, one of the first books he ever gave me was Engels's "Origin of the family". Clearly he didn't think my book was rubbish or he wouldn't have wasted his time typing it. (I once tried to write a novel and he took that line with it. When I came across the manuscript of the first pages years later, I saw at a glance that he had been dead right, and had saved me from wasting a lot of time.) Maybe some of Engels' ideas had sunk into my head though I hadn't been aware of it. He had written, for example, that "the tribes which figure in books as living entirely, i. e. exclusively, by hunting never existed in reality: the yield of the hunt was far too precarious."

People who read the book sometimes asked me: "But how did you know all that stuff?" Well, I had three years of Oxford under my belt and it teaches you how to find things out. And in the years while I was waiting for someone else to write a response to "The Naked Ape" I had read a lot of the background material simply trying to find answers to questions. The biggest one was this: I was convinced that our earliest ancestors had not been well adapted for life on the plains – but if not there, then where? I had been intrigued when I came across a brief reference in Desmond's book to Sir Alister Hardy, who had asked, in an article in the New Scientist: "Was Man more aquatic in the past?" His question had been ignored for twelve years and largely forgotten, but I found it blindingly illuminating and now I picked it up and ran with it.

I wrote to Sir Alister telling him I thought of writing a book in support of the aquatic theme, in case he had found further arguments in its favour in the intervening twelve years that he might be willing to share. His first answer was very kind – he was a very kind man – but guarded. He had not given up hope of writing more extensively on the subject himself and was keeping a notebook to that end. Not long afterwards, another letter arrived, saying that he had been advised that a popular book on the subject might be a good thing. It would arouse interest in the subject and make it easier to find a publisher for the more scholarly version that he might ultimately produce. So I could go ahead with his blessing.

When the book was finished I sent it to Harvey Unna. Two days later he rang me, sounding kind of stunned. "You…?" he said. "You just sat down and wrote that book?" All his instincts told him it would be a bestseller and he was right. Nine different countries commissioned translations of it in the first year. I rang up Alister and told him that the book was going to be published. He was interested and pleased and asked the name of it. When I told him, there was a long silence. "The descent of *what?*" he asked. I realised I had never mentioned that angle. I could only hope it hadn't come as too much of a shock.

Souvenir Press bought the rights to it and Stein and Day in New York issued the American edition. Sol Stein came over to meet me. He would like to make plans for a coast-to-coast promotional tour but he wanted to take a look at me first. He had learned I was a Welsh housewife aged 52 and that didn't sound very promising for prime-time television. But he decided I was up to it. The Observer arranged to serialise passages from the book on two consecutive Sundays, and arrangements for the American tour went ahead. Somebody has commented that there was once a time when an author could write "Go, little book…" and send it on its way into the wide world, but nowadays he has to go with it. By 1972 both Dylan and Gareth were at university, Dylan at Oxford and Gareth at Aberystwyth, but Huw was still at school and would have had to come home to an empty house until Morien returned. It would have been awkward in various ways, so I asked Stein and Day if I could bring a boy with me – I would pay his expenses. They agreed. (The courier who met me in the airport later told me she had been relieved to see him. They had envisioned that I meant a toy boy, and that didn't fit the image they were promoting.) The other good thing in that first day or two was a telegram from Sir Alister who had read the book and said "Brilliant." So that was one worry off my mind.

We were put up in the poshest hotels. Huw was happy flipping through all the tv channels and ordering food by room service, and volunteers took him to see the sights if I had to be away all day. We had just one whole day off together – Sunday – and spent it in Disneyland. After the first tour I was invited back for another one, omitting California this time but taking in bigger chunks of the Middle West where I got cross-questioned by fundamentalists more interested in the God angle than in either feminism or Hardyism. On chat shows I met celebrities like comedian Mort Sahl and film star Raquel Welsh and Leonard Nimoy who played Spock in Star Trek.

Why was the book so successful? There's no blinking the fact that some of it was due to the fact that sex came into the book. It wasn't shoved in as an optional extra: it was a serious integral part of the thesis, confronting questions like why is a man's penis bigger than a gorilla's? But the book had other things going for it too. The timing couldn't have been better. When I was writing *The Descent of Woman*, Germaine Greer was writing *The Female Eunuch*. The phenomenon that came to be known as Women's Lib was just taking off, so there was a hungry audience waiting for this kind of message. The third factor was a stroke of pure luck. Just as I set out for America, the pundits who chose the U. S. Book of the Month found themselves in a quandary. They had decided to select a biography of the millionaire recluse Howard Hughes. This publishing event had been eagerly awaited because he had always previously refused to give interviews or talk about his past, but at the last moment it was discovered that the new biography was a hoax, so there was a crisis. The best thing they could find at short notice to replace it was *The Descent of Woman*.

In some of the chat shows I went on, the interviewer would be male and hostile. One had done a bit of research and found I had three children. As he was winding up the discussion he drew a graphic picture of where all this talk of equality was leading. Here was I flaunting myself in the public eye, and meantime my hapless henpecked spouse was abandoned, struggling to cope with the three little ones all on his own. Was this the kind of future we wanted for the human race? I just had time to put him right before the end-titles rolled.

More unexpectedly, I got some flak from the feminists too. Gloria Steinem invited me to the offices of MS magazine. The atmosphere there was quite exciting. There was a feeling of great solidarity and self-confidence and an absolute conviction that things were changing in the right direction and changing fast. It was true, and I rejoiced in it, but they were not at all sure about me. I was of the wrong generation – the same age as the mothers of most of them. That was the generation they were rebelling against. Their mothers had meekly submitted to male domination, accepted the stifling bonds of matrimony and tried to bring up their daughters to conform to it too. But they would have none of it. Down with the nuclear family! Down with men. We don't need them. "A woman without a man is like a fish without a bicycle."

Also I was talking about evolution, and in their experience any talk about the biological differences between the sexes led to the conclusion that the way society was at present organised was irrevocably laid down in our genes: it could never change. I have never believed that for a moment – it was one of the things I was out to challenge – but some of them felt that Darwin was not on their side, and it was safer not to be lured into talking about him. The general feeling was that I was not on-message. I was saying that we were the equals of men. That was okay as far as it went, but I was failing to point out that the reverse was not true: they were not our equals, they were *worse* than us.

After the tour, Alister invited me to Oxford. I had never met him, and his wife had no idea what to expect. She had been disturbed by recent events. They revived memories of unhappier days that she had hoped were gone forever. When he published his article in 1960, there had been furious reactions from his colleagues. They felt that he had let them all down by publishing such a patently absurd idea, and exposing Oxford academia to ridicule, more especially since he was not an anthropologist at all, but merely a marine biologist. He was not entitled to hold bizarre opinions on other people's specialities and certainly not to go public with them. Some of them had been incandescent, and virtually no one had been on his side.

And now she feared it was all happening again. Television people had come and interviewed Alister and followed him around with a camera. He had been allowed to speak his mind, was respectfully listened to, and had quite enjoyed it, but some of their oldest friends were shaking their heads and offering her silent sympathy. One of her close friends was Professor Katy Lee, from Lady Margaret Hall, who had been my tutor and was also invited to tea, ready to supply moral support if necessary. Alister was a lovely man who wouldn't hurt a fly, and I tried hard to convey that I didn't want to hurt a fly either. Miss Lee made a few comments on the book just as if it was still 1939 and I had submitted it for a tutorial, but apart from that we didn't talk science at all. We simply enjoyed a pleasant afternoon.

And then it was all over and life returned to normal. Women's Lib went from strength to strength under the leadership of younger and more focussed women, and any contribution I might have made that summer to the process of consciousness-raising was soon forgotten. The aquatic concept – that an aquatic interlude may have led to most of the differences between apes and humans – was treated in exactly the same way that Hardy's original suggestion had been treated. There was dead silence on that front for the next ten years. Obviously it was still regarded by professional scientists as too stupid an idea even to merit a reply. My book was just amateur populist stuff and they had their own busy lives to get on with.

And so had I. It had been an exhilarating interlude. It had slaked any stirrings of wanderlust – which had never been all that powerful anyway – and I was back home, and there were some interesting suggestions coming in from the BBC. There was talk of a new genre – the biopic. That meant dramatisations of the lives of real people, requiring some talent for research as well as imagination and an ear for period dialogue. Would I be interested in that? You bet I would. It was right up my street.

CHAPTER 15

Flying High

In the decade following the publication of the book I continued to write plays, series, and adaptations. Actually, I also published one more book in the seventies. It was called *Falling Apart*, and it was about urbanisation, but it sank without trace. I bit off more than I could chew that time. Socio-economics is a vast subject, and it would be advisable to soak yourself in it for about five years before piping up. So I went on writing for television – chiefly, though not exclusively, for the BBC. In the beginning it had been for BBC Wales, but later all the commissions were coming from London. I had to go up there fairly frequently – once every month or two – and the question again began to be raised: Wouldn't it be more convenient to move up there?

I never wanted to, and it wouldn't have been practicable anyway. My job could be done anywhere but Morien's couldn't. He loved his job and was very good at it: he had been appointed in an advisory capacity as Head of Languages for schools throughout the area. He also played a much bigger part in the local community than I did. He had joined the Labour Party in Aberdare. It had been barely solvent when he joined. He arranged for it to buy a building to be known as the Labour Rooms, so that it would have a base to operate from, and could let out rooms on the premises to other local organisations needing a venue for weekly meetings. It could also be hired for special occasions like weddings and anniversaries, and before long it was running at a profit. He belonged to a trade union and sometimes had to go to London himself in that capacity. He ran a chess club. He was still doing all my typing. He was active in CND and organised a Ban the Bomb week in Aberdare with a whole range of meetings and visiting speakers and other events. He was a man that people came to when they were in trouble. He found a sculptor to design a plaque for the Aberdare library commemorating the International Brigaders who died in Spain. He featured on tv in a series made in Wales called "The Colliers' Crusade." A man from the War Office Museum heard that he had written an account of his experiences in the Spanish Civil War, and asked if they could have it for their archives. While he was there I mentioned Billy's account of the first world war, and he took that too.

I once heard a man say an extraordinary thing about him. He said if he was hanging over a cliff and somebody at the top of it was leaning over holding his hand, he would hope it would be Morien Morgan.

Clearly, as long as we stuck together and stayed put we made a good team. I was getting pretty good at scriptwriting by that time, but I wouldn't have been able to keep up such a high rate of output if the nature of the market had not changed. One of the first things you have to do as a playwright is to think of an idea – a situation, a plot, a storyline. It is usually sparked off by something in your own experience, involving the kinds of people and relationships you have known, however cleverly disguised by changing the place, time, and background. Once you've come up with a dozen or so plots of that kind, it gets much harder to think of something fresh. In my experience it doesn't pay to carry on doing other things while waiting for the Muse to present you with a sudden flash of inspiration. Somebody described writing as the art of applying the seat of the pants to the seat of the chair, and there is some truth in that.

Adaptations are much easier: you get presented with the subject matter. I wrote half a dozen episodes of the popular *Maigret* series, some based on novels that had not been translated into English, but French was Morien's speciality and that helped. I wrote nine episodes of an even more popular series, called *Dr. Finlay's Casebook*. It was based on characters created by A. J. Cronin. The few stories he wrote about them were quickly used up, and from then on, writers were expected to come up with their own plots. I enjoyed writing those. They were set in a period I had lived through, and were located in the Celtic Fringe of the UK, where I felt at home.

The place was Scotland instead of Wales, but I soaked myself in Lewis Grassic Gibbons's "*A Scots Quair*" and evolved a kind of dialect I thought of as Basic British. (They still kept a Scotsman on hand to vet the scripts, in case phrases or cadences of South Wales English ever contaminated them.) Within the familiar precincts of the fictional town of Tannochbrae you could freely dramatise issues that would elsewhere have raised eyebrows, such as euthanasia or venereal disease, and nobody ever complained, although they went out on Sunday evenings. I even invented one incident in which a real life character, Willie Gallagher, dropped in at the Tannochbrae surgery. In his lifetime he had been the Communist MP for West Fife, and his family wrote me a letter saying how surprised and moved they had been by that episode.

By the seventies, demand was also growing for adaptations of historical novels and dramatisations of the lives of real people. Oxford had given me a good ear for period dialogue, necessary in adapting nineteenth century novels like "Mary Barton."

Then in 1975 the BBC decided to televise "How Green Was My Valley." At first I heard nothing about those plans. I had the qualifications to write such an adaptation. In fact I knew more about the reality of the time and place it depicted than the author himself, because my father-in-law Johnnie Morgan had been there in the thick of it, and I could read his diaries. Nevertheless, I was not the first choice. They wanted a really big name for it. They wanted Emlyn Williams, and he was willing to consider it. To me Emlyn was a hero. In 1940 his play "The Corn is Green" had been a great success in the West End. I'd never seen it performed but I'd got it out of the library and been excited by it and it was one of the things that had made me think of playwriting as a possible thing to do. Emlyn's plays had been spectacular hits on Broadway. Actresses from Ethel Barrymore in 1940 to Bette Davies and Katherine Hepburn had starred in them and Hollywood made "Night Must Fall" into a movie not once but twice, in 1937 and 1964.

And yet somehow it didn't turn out as planned. For 45 years, Emlyn had been steeped in the requirements of the Theatre, and he knew those requirements like the back of his hand. In a big auditorium most of the audience can't see the expressions that flicker in the eyes of an actor. That's why body language on the stage can sometimes convey more than facial expressions. It's also why everything has to be put into words, more so than in everyday life, and more so than on television. Reactions to a stage play are greatly magnified through being experienced by a captive audience, hundreds of people sitting in the dark in the same place, because under those conditions the emotions are as contagious as laughter can be. In some subtle way the grammar is different when your audience is fragmented into groups of one or two, free to comment to one another and have a giggle, or wander out and make a cup of tea.

In those days if asked to fill in "profession" I always wrote "playwright" rather than "dramatist". For me the word "drama" was associated with the stage, and laden with centuries of literary tradition going back to Ancient Greece. Nobody thought of writing for the telly as literature. I did attempt one or two little stage plays for local groups, and Harvey Unna once sold a play of mine, originally written for television, as a stage production, presented at the Vaudeville Theatre. But it didn't work and only ran for three weeks. It was not my scene.

In a similar way, perhaps, television wasn't Emlyn's. It's possible that a script editor might have felt hesitant about suggesting a re-write of any passage sent in by a world-famous writer. It's equally possible that Emlyn found he didn't enjoy applying his mind to characters and situations he didn't invent and couldn't modify. I don't know what happened or who blinked first. For whatever reason, they found themselves with the dates pencilled in for "How Green" to be screened, rehearsal date looming uncomfortably close, and no scripts that everyone was entirely happy with. They turned to the old hoss. One of the lessons I'd learned was how to work fast and meet deadlines. Denis Norden has vividly described the response given to writers pleading for just a little bit more time to get it right: "No. We don't want it right. We want it Tuesday." So I spat on my hands and got down to it, and met the deadline. All the cast were Welsh, and they loved making it, and the viewing figures were terrific.

When I went up for the screening of some of these programmes I occasionally met people who had been invited to attend because they had some connection with the subjects of the programmes. After writing "For the Love of Egypt" I met the grandchildren of Flinders Petrie; after writing "Testament of Youth" I met the housekeeper who had looked after Vera Britain and Winifred Holtby; after "The Life and Times of David Lloyd George" I met the man who for years been his private secretary, and after dramatising "The Diary of Anne Frank" I met a woman who had been at school with her.

While researching for the pilot episode of an ITV series called "Sanctuary", I spent a few days in a convent to get the feel of the place. It was a working order – the Sisters of Charity of St. Vincent de Paul – and many of them had jobs to go to during the day. I'd read novels by Catholics (male) who'd been taught by nuns, and walloped by them, and those books painted grim pictures of them. And of course I didn't believe what they believed. But the convent in London struck me as quite a busy and cheerful and musical place – they had guitars, as well as an organ. They didn't seem to me to feel deprived or bored or solemn or sanctimonious. While I was there, one old nun came back from a fortnight's "retreat" and I was moved by the spontaneously warm welcome that greeted her return. Not a bad place to grow old in – you'll never lack care and company. On the subject of nuns, I once met Mother Teresa too, in Rome, when the BBC was briefly exploring the possibility of producing a series on her life.

Emerging after that brief encounter, I found myself standing outside the convent, miles away from my hotel in Rome, on a long white road stretching to the horizon in both directions, and the taxi-driver who had brought me there had taken the last of my supply of Italian currency. For want of any better idea, I started to walk. After ten minutes, a bus appeared. I held out my hand and it stopped and I got on it. Time went by. Nobody asked me for the fare. It seemed uncannily like supernatural intervention, but I was later told that the communists then running Rome had decreed free travel for the workers. In the end, the Mother Teresa series was never made. She had promised the film rights to a Catholic writer in America, who planned to make a film about her, and now declared that the terms of that agreement precluded her from co-operating with any other media project. So she wrote to me and asked me to drop the idea.

Another intensely interesting project was when I was asked to write about the life of Joey Deacon, the spastic who was for years thought incapable of speech. He made unintelligible sounds, until one day a new inmate answered him. The newcomer's speech was impaired, but not so badly. He was the only one who could understand what Joey was trying to say, and he began to act as his interpreter. A third inmate was able to type, and between the three of them they slowly wrote Joey's life story and it was published. And the tv documentary based on it won the Prix Italia.

Adapters tended to become typecast. I was chosen to write the story of Gwen John, possibly because of the Welsh connection, and later the life of Stanley Spencer, perhaps because having written about one painter I could be trusted with another one. Also, maybe on the strength of my book, I was invited to write about scientists. I wrote "The Forgotten Voyage" about Alfred Russell Wallace, "The Garden of Inheritance" about Gregor Mendel, and a 5-part life of Marie Curie that won a Bafta award for the Best Drama serial of 1977. Throughout most of that time I was too busy to spend much time thinking about the putative aquatic origins of *Homo sapiens*. I thought I'd exhausted what I had to say on the subject and that chapter of my life was now closed. How wrong can you be?

There was an American policeman living in Reno. Years later he and his wife visited us in Mountain Ash, but I never did learn much about his life, though I do remember one anecdote he told me. He was keeping watch over some building that had been carefully prepared and vetted for an important meeting the next day, when he heard sounds in a corridor. He knew that nobody in Reno had any right to be anywhere in that building at that time, so he went to investigate, saw two men some way ahead of him and gave chase. One of them turned and asked: "You're not going to put me in the slammer, are you?" It was John Kennedy.

The policeman was Chuck Milliken. He had read *The Descent of Woman*. The feminist theme left him cold, but he was totally convinced by the Hardy theory and waited for somebody to respond to it, or for me to follow it up. Neither of those things happened, and he lost patience. He began writing to people who had published books about evolution, and professors in various universities who took courses in evolution, asking them if they were aware of this idea and what they thought of it. Most of them predictably didn't reply, and the ones who did generally pointed out that the author of the book in question was not a scientist, and no one with any knowledge of the subject took it seriously.

He also kept writing to me, and sending some of the letters he'd received, and pointing out that none of them were giving him any proper answers, and demanding to know why I wasn't doing something about it. I *ought* to do something about it. I couldn't just leave things the way they were. It was a wake-up call, and it finally became loud enough to induce me to take time off tv and write a little book. I owe Chuck Milliken a debt of gratitude.

At that time Alister was still alive, and quite ready to co-operate. He wrote a preface to my second book, *The Aquatic Ape,* and his photograph appeared at the beginning of it. There was not much that was new in it, but it served three purposes. It demolished the idea that some people had been circulating: that Alister had floated the idea as a joke, and I'd been stupid enough to take it seriously. It presented it as a free-standing proposition, not mixed up with feminism or politics. And thirdly, it made accessible in one volume all that he himself had actually written on the subject – the New Scientist article of 22 years earlier, and one or two later pieces, and a paper by Leon LaLumiere that Hardy thought highly of and had read into the proceedings of the Royal Society.

As for me, writing it had wiped out the wimpish doubts that had taken root in my mind. I had come to suspect that it was just possible, after all, that the conventional wisdom subscribed to by all the brightest and best of the established scientists might be right, and I might be wrong. Now, having caught up on a lot of stuff that had been written in the intervening ten years, I felt more strongly than ever that they were on the wrong track.

CHAPTER 16

Changing Track

When I published the Aquatic Ape I was 62. At that age, if you've got an established career and you're enjoying it, you can reasonably expect to keep going for several more years. And I did actually do that. I continued writing for the BBC, and in the next six years I sold another two serials, and eight more one-off biopics, and a radio play about George Bernard Shaw.

It would be nice to claim that I then retired leaving them wanting more – that's what people in showbiz are always urged to do. It wouldn't be true though. After thirty years, it was no longer an asset to have been in at the beginning: too many things had changed. Techniques had changed. The audience's expectations had changed and their attention span had shortened. Different people were in charge and used very different criteria for judging a script. Competition with other channels, once non-existent, was now exerting powerful pressures. Drama took up a much smaller percentage of screen time because game shows were cheaper, and there were scores of up-and-coming young writers hell-bent on getting a foothold. All those are hand-waving explanations for the fact that I was coming to the end of my shelf life in television.

Something else was happening too. It was as if – I find this hard to explain – as if my mind had a mind of its own. It was still capable of turning out a script, but it needed coaxing ("Come on, concentrate, you know you can do this"), instead of sliding into the job like a seal into water. And every day, as soon as I'd achieved seven or eight hundred words of dialogue and let it off the hook, it heaved a sigh of relief. Work was over and it could now go out to play, as I picked up a book by S. J. Gould or Richard Dawkins or Peter Medawar or Frans de Waal or E. O. Wilson or whoever. One day it occurred to me with a slight shock that I hadn't read a novel in the last twelve months. This other stuff was far more riveting.

So I began going more deeply into the questions surrounding human evolution. I no longer needed prompting from Chuck. This subject moved to the top of my agenda and I had a lot of catching up to do. I began attending conferences – I would go anywhere to learn about it and/or talk about it. Some of the places and universities in which I attended academic events in later years included, in alphabetic order: Berkeley, Boston, Cambridge, Cardiff, Ghent, Harvard, Heidelberg, Lampeter, Liverpool, London, Oxford, San Francisco, Rutgers, South Africa, Toronto, Southampton, Switzerland, and Valkenberg. And I wrote books. In 1990, aged seventy, I published "The Scars of Evolution" and four years after that "The Descent of the Child" and three years after that "The Aquatic Ape Hypothesis". There were, later, two other books that publishers wouldn't look at but I published them anyway. "Pinker's List" was a mix of science and politics. "The Naked Darwinist" was a brief summary of the road I had travelled in promoting Hardy's heresy, and the responses I received. I am not going to try to summarise here the twists and turns of the arguments for and against the aquatic theory. But it might be of interest to try to convey the flavour of what it was like living through those days, and recall some of the incidents that have stuck in my memory.

I remember, for example, the first time I met David Attenborough. It was on the eve of the first of the superb series of "Life" programmes that have continued ever since, and will always be reckoned as the BBC's finest contributions to public understanding of the world we live in. The Radio Times commissioned me to interview him and write an introduction to the first series "Life on Earth." His first words to me as he opened the door were: "I know who *you* are!" I had read up all I could about him so that I could ask intelligent questions. All of it was intriguing and impressive and often entertaining. I remember reading, for instance, about the incident when the BBC's crew sent a wireless message ahead to some far-flung tropical island, alerting them about who would be arriving there in a couple of days with his entourage. When they landed they were greeted with the kind of welcome suitable for a royal consort. Wireless reception was not very good there and "Attenborough" can sound very much like "Edinburgh".

That meeting with David is a very happy memory – his wife was from Wales, and had made some Welsh cakes to make me feel at home – and it may have helped in some small way to get me out of a very frustrating situation a few years later. This arose in connection with the British Association for the Advancement of Science, as it had been known since its foundation in 1831 – it's now been renamed the British Science Association. In preparation for its annual week of promoting greater public interest in science, it announced that anyone at all could come and take part, and stage their own event, as long as they organised it themselves and paid any expenses that might be incurred. I drew up a list of contributors, including Michael Crawford, Marc Verhaegen, and Michel Odent, made sure they were all available and willing to attend, prepared some film clips and posters, and submitted an application.

It was turned down. Apparently the aquatic theory was not regarded as science. There was no appeal. I'd have to write around and say: "Sorry, it's all off." But the BAAS was in the habit of annually appointing some public figure to serve as its president for one year. The president for that year was David Attenborough. Quite by accident he came to hear of our application and argued that we were simply putting forward a tenable idea for discussion and debate, and he could see no grounds for denying it a hearing. So we were in. And the President attended one of our sessions.

Another memorable meeting was at Oxford, where I had been invited to speak to the Anthropological Society. That was where I first heard about the Internet. Douglas Adams, author of the *Hitchhiker's Guide to the Galaxy*, had come to the meeting. He was keenly interested in AAT. After the meeting, during the usual social gathering over drinks and nibbles, he told me about this new channel of communication called the Internet and urged me to get acquainted with it, as it would be the quickest way of making the idea known to a wider range of people.

As soon as I got home, I followed his advice. It changed my life in the way it changed so many people's lives. The new medium was in its first days and the people involved in it were predominantly young and raw and male and geeky. I found a group discussing anthropology, but I didn't find a welcome. Several of them kept urging me to shut up and get out of their air space. They hadn't read the book. I didn't at first realise that they assumed this Elaine person was some snooty young female trying to show off and upstage them and they weren't having it. I only realised what they'd been thinking when one of them came across an e-mail sent to a different group by my *grandson*. Wow!!! The implication then was that I'd been deliberately cagey about my date of birth (it had never occurred to me to mention it) and they'd succeeded in blowing my cover. Instead of interpreting my suggestions as the prattling of an uppity co-ed, they could now be dismissed as the mumblings of an aged crone.

Luckily this initial mix-up didn't last long. As more and more people joined the group, it became possible to discuss the arguments in depth. I was able to glean references to recent papers and titles of textbooks that I'd otherwise never heard of, and that helped me to compensate for not having studied science at university. Some of the interchanges were quite heated but others were really constructive. Misunderstandings were ironed out, source materials shared, inaccurate assertions withdrawn or modified. Only one online correspondent, the redoubtable Jim Moore, has made it his life's work not simply to disagree with AAT, but to use the Internet to warn the world of my personal perfidy, deliberate lies, and evil intent, as he continues to do down to the present day.

A conference held in Valkenberg in 1987 was one of the most absorbing and satisfying events I had ever attended. It was the only time when well-qualified people on both sides of the controversy came together and seriously addressed the issues at length, in detail, with conviction but without hostility. I got the impression that everyone enjoyed the experience. The views put forward were subsequently put on record in a book entitled "The Aquatic Ape: Fact or Fiction?"

Even more exciting was the week-long conference organised in South Africa to celebrate the end of the cultural embargo which had isolated South African scientists from their colleagues during the years of apartheid. It was attended by delegates from all over the world and covered all aspects of human evolution. I have vivid memories of the moment when Phillip Tobias lifted off the glass dome protecting the Taung skull and allowed me to hold it in my hands. For many years this object, first described by Raymond Dart in 1924, was the most famous and controversial fossil in the world. It was the first piece of evidence confirming Darwin's hunch that the human story might have begun in Africa.

Another excursion full of happy memories was a visit to Boston. Daniel Dennett, at Tufts University, had conceived an interesting idea for a series of six weekly meetings on different aspects of science. He drew up a list of six women who would present unorthodox ideas that they were trying to promote despite encountering varying degrees of resistance. I was one of them. He met me at the airport and welcomed me cordially. I remember the drive from the aiport in an open car in the breezy sunshine, and from the very first moment swapping questions and answers and ideas with him as freely as if we had been friends for years.

The meeting was well attended. I'm sure some of those present – for all I know the majority – had come for the entertainment value, to confirm their assumption that this woman was as nutty as a fruitcake. But I could see the expressions on some of their faces change in the course of the talk. I certainly wouldn't claim to have converted anybody, but I think I convinced them that I was drawing attention to some pertinent questions that had nobody had yet answered. The first to respond was an old gentleman who rose at the end of the talk quivering with outrage, and passionately denounced the whole idea of allowing me to enter those hallowed walls to spout such perfidy and misleading statements. Dan told me later that he'd been momentarily alarmed in case I might be upset by this, and wondered whether he should intervene. It was unnecessary. By that time, I had been denounced and derided by masters of the polemic art over a period of years, both on line and off it. I replied with the utmost respect and courtesy and he sat down.

While I was in Boston, I had the privilege of staying overnight with Lynn Margulis, whose first paper on the origin of eukaryotic organelles had been rejected by the first fifteen scientific journals she sent it to. It has now long been recognised as a landmark in modern endosymbiotic theory. I also had the privilege of being conducted around Tecumseh Fitch's laboratory. It was like a small museum, with glass cases of specimens, and newly equipped with the very latest in magnetic resonance imaging at a time when MRI was a brand new technology. One thing he mentioned in passing, which I have never forgotten, was that one day he had gone down to the beach and found the dead bodies of a number of cormorants lying there, and every one of them had the tail end of a fish sticking out of its mouth. My guess is that a shoal of those fish had for some reason swum into those waters and the cormorants welcomed the bonanza without realising that they were a size larger than their accustomed prey. That would be fatal, because having begun the process of swallowing they were unable to regurgitate, and with their mouths blocked they would very quickly suffocate. Like several species of diving birds they have no nostrils.

Spreading the word led me to places I would never otherwise have seen. One meeting was held in a dazzlingly beautiful venue in the Alps. My visit there was sponsored by Robert Martin, who had known Hardy and was his friend. In 1972, when the AAT story first broke, television programme-makers had been very keen to find any scientist willing to discuss it on air. Those opposed to Hardy preserved a solid front of non-participation: it was too silly to waste their time on. I don't know whether Hardy contacted Martin, but as far I remember he was the only scientist who agreed to cooperate in making a tv programme about it, not committing himself either way but explaining in clear and simple terms what was being suggested, and the arguments for and against it.

He introduced the meeting in Switzerland in the same vein: "Here is something you might consider worth thinking about." After I'd spoken, one elderly scholar rose to his feet, and just like his counterpart in Boston passionately condemned the decision to allow me to air such views.

During the visit to Switzerland, there was plenty of opportunity to discuss all aspects of the question with Robert Martin. I remember at one point suggesting that pectoral mammary glands – i. e. nipples on the chest instead of in rows as in pigs, or at the back end of the body as in cows and horses – were a sure sign that there had been an arboreal ancestor somewhere in the family tree. He said: "Ah!" – he'd never considered the point – and held up his finger while he mentally, at great speed, riffled through his encyclopaedic knowledge of mammalian anatomy. Then he said: "No" with such conviction that I knew he'd thought of an animal that disproved the possibility. I later regretted not asking him what it was. Perhaps it was the elephant.

At one point I was waiting with his wife in their house in Zurich for him to come back from another appointment, and I discovered to my delight that they were currently acting as the custodians of a young orang-utan and he was being treated more or less like one of the family. I enjoyed the opportunity of playing with him for the best part of an hour. He was old enough to clamber over the furniture and shake hands and explore his environment in various ways. The thing that struck me most forcibly was that I could never induce him to make eye contact. Dogs and cats readily make eye contact with humans. They instinctively look into our faces, rather than at our arms or kneecaps, to divine what we're likely to do next. The young orang refused to do anything of the kind. He's the only ape I've ever been properly introduced to, and I sometimes wonder whether all apes are like that, or whether that one might have been slightly autistic.

I hope I have made it clear that although I encountered active hostility, especially in the early days, the most heated attacks always came from people who were no better qualified than I was. The professionals, almost without exception were very kind, even if they were totally convinced I was mistaken. When I met any of them – for example when Leslie Aiello invited me to UCL, or Robert Foley invited me to Cambridge – the welcome was warm and the discussions were lively and I learned a lot from them.

After the first years, I was only one among a growing number of people who found the general idea credible and made invaluable contributions to it. For example, Michael Crawford examined the nutritional aspects and the particular relevance, especially to the growing brain, of the balance of Omega 3 and Omega 6 found in the sea food chain. Erika Schagatay's career had begun by visiting the dwindling number of tribes whose subsistence depended on fishing rather than hunting, and she went on to specialise in researching the diving reflex. Michel Odent was drawn to it by his interest in water birthing. Marc Verhaegen was an early supporter of the basic theory. He still strongly supports the idea of an aquatic influence on our evolutionary history, but has constructed a revised scenario: in place of the Hardy/Morgan thesis he envisages an aquatic episode taking place at the time when the apes split from the monkeys. Renato Bender researched the work of European scientists like Max von Westenhofer who had speculated on a possible aquatic ancestor before Hardy, though Hardy died without ever suspecting that he had been forestalled. Algis Kuliukas has concentrated on researching the evidence for the belief that wading behaviour offers the most convincing explanation of the emergence of bipedalism. Stephen Cunnane's book "Survival of the Fattest" explores how the distribution of adipose tissue in humans differs from that of apes.

In 1995, Philip Tobias first published his conviction that the savannah theory would have to be abandoned, and when he celebrated the end of apartheid in his country by staging in South Africa a week-long conference of evolutionary scientists from all over the world, a few of us were invited to attend. Some of the proceedings were filmed and featured in the Discovery Channel's documentary programme "The Aquatic Ape".

There are many others who have given valuable support. By now the list of supporters and contributors runs into hundreds and the concept has spread around the world. In 2000 I was awarded the Letten Saugstad prize in Oslo. Books written about it have appeared in translation in Japanese and more recently in Chinese. Last week I received a complimentary copy of a book printed in Russian with my name in the index. Meanwhile, here in Britain I became conscious of a palpable change in people's perceptions of the aquatic theory after Sir David Attenborough had presented two programmes about it on BBC radio in consecutive weeks. After that, you might disagree with it, but you can bet nobody's going to laugh it off.

The year before last I was invited to give a talk at a TED conference. They were taking a chance: I was in my 89th year and the room was packed with mainly young people looking for vibrant new ideas for the future. I clambered onto the platform with my walking stick. I had been given permission to deliver the talk sitting down. The audience had no idea what to expect and I had no idea how they would receive it, but I did know this would have to be my swan song. A voice from seventy years earlier whispered in my ear: "Knock 'em cold, kid!" and I listened to it. And it all went like a dream, and I got a standing ovation.

So one way and another I've had a fortunate life, full of interest and full of surprises. In this account of it, as in most autobiographies – I would guess 100% – there are incidents I've forgotten, and others I've omitted because I prefer to forget them, or because they impinge on other people's privacy. I think that last consideration may be the reason why most autobiographies don't, for example, go into details about the life and times of their children and in-laws and grandchildren, and I'm not going to do that either. But perhaps, to wind things up, I should give some brief indication of the way things are now.

I'm still in Mountain Ash. Morien died in 1997. Towards the end of his life his health was not good. He was diagnosed as diabetic and put on steroids. He was taken to hospital after falling and breaking his hip, and never recovered. In the last weeks he was moved to the local Mountain Ash hospital at the bottom of this street, only five minutes away. The nurses were kind, and tolerant, and flexible about visiting hours. I was allowed to go in after he'd had a meal and he was then permitted one cigarette, as long as I was there to ensure it wouldn't drop and set the bedclothes alight. By then he had nothing to lose, and there was nothing else he craved, so I felt they were being humane in permitting it. On my last visit he was asleep. He opened his eyes and said, with a kind of amusement: "Still here, then?" I don't think he meant me. I think he meant himself – he'd gone to sleep the night before not expecting to wake up, and fully accepting that. I hope I will be able to end as peacefully.

I won't pretend our marriage hadn't been through one or two turbulent patches, and the fact that it survived them doesn't qualify me to hand out any advice on relationships. The strongest factor determining the outcome was one it would be impossible to reproduce, namely getting married in the first half of the twentieth century. Fewer people today go into a partnership with the firm conviction that this thing is going to have to last until death us do part. Nor would I claim to know whether the loosening of the bonds makes things better or worse. Better in some respects, worse in others.

I was seventy-seven when Morien died. There weren't many people left in my life of my own generation, and none of the previous one. Olive had died in 1981, after suffering from Alzheimer's disease. She had, by then, been widowed for a second time. I will always be immensely grateful that my school friend Priscilla, a qualified nurse, was willing to move in to live with her and care for her towards the end. I used to take over every weekend to give her a break.

After Morien's death I had a lot to learn. My typing was (still is) an inelegant two-finger process. For a period Judith Hayes, in California, volunteered to take over the job of keeping track of what I was writing, and turn it into an elegantly laid out final product. She is a militant secularist with a sense of humour, and the author of a book entitled "The Happy Heretic". She saved the situation at one point when my aged computer had a nervous breakdown and wouldn't spew out anything but alphabet soup. An almost-finished book had vanished beyond recall, but Judith had preserved it. She also researched and compiled the lists in the appendix.

The three sons turned out very differently. Dylan was academically brilliant. He went to Jesus College, Oxford and got a first in mathematics. He served as Senior Scientific Officer at the Royal Aircraft Establishment and conducted research in the Mathematics Department of Dundee University. Later, though he retained an interest in that field and continued to publish occasional papers, he decided to make a radical change of direction and became a hypnotherapist. I think there had been parts of his nature that weren't being used: he had great warmth and empathy and those qualities hadn't had much chance to express themselves. He was successful in both careers. He died suddenly, to my great grief and that of many other people, last year.

Gareth was a child of the sixties. He won a scholarship to Aberystwyth but halfway through his course he happened to encounter some roving American hippies. Like many other young people at that time, he suddenly dropped out, turned on, and took off, wandering the world making love not war, and showing up at rare intervals to say hello and stay for a few days. He reminds me of Billy in many ways – not much interested in gathering moss, but very ingenious at making and mending and building things. If ever he felt the need of cash he could always instantly earn some without being tied down to anything as stultifying as a career. He has finally settled in Corfu, as he had determined to do very early in life after reading Gerald Durrell's book "My Family and Other Animals", and he comes over for a visit about twice a year. Huw Morien was the one who settled in this area and never wanted to leave it. That's been lucky for me, because some time after Morien's death he moved back into this house and now lives upstairs with his partner while I live on the ground floor. He is a support worker, and she is an occupational health nurse, and this arrangement works well for all of us. Scattered around in Scotland, Texas, and the North of England I have one grandson, two granddaughters, and one great-grandson.

I'm now ninety-one, hard of hearing, unsteady on my feet, and my sight isn't what it was. I have the predictable difficulties with remembering people's names, and what day of the week it is, and what I came into this room to look for. But I still do the *Guardian* cryptic crossword and for some years I've been writing a weekly column for the *Western Mail*. I've been very lucky that my life has lasted so long without ever becoming boring, and I've enjoyed telling you about it.

As they say on the air: "Thank you for listening."

Postscript

(for those who may still be interested)

1. What's happening to the water theory?

It has gained numerous supporters over the years. The awareness of it continues to grow, and spread to new parts of the world. A recent e-book entitled "Was Msn more aquatic in the past?" illustrated the breadth of its appeal to specialists in different fields, and the kinds of evidence on which it is based.

Since the savannah theory was tacitly abandoned, no new paradigm has been advanced to explain why one of the apes evolved into a naked biped.

Among supporters of the water theory, there is frequently vigorous disagreement over the exact nature and location and timing of the hypothesised aquatic interlude.

Such heated debates are often a reliable indication of work in progress, and have often preceded new solutions that resolve the differences and lead to a new consensus.

2. What's happening to Darwinism?

In recent years a new generation of scientists has transformed the study of evolution by exploiting new technologies in the fields of genetics, embryology and epigenetics. These researchers are daily enlarging our understanding. The work is exciting, productive, generously funded, and inevitably attracts the highest proportion of the most ambitious students hoping to make a name for themselves. One of the most eloquent, charismatic and intrepid exponents of this new approach is Aaron Filler, whose ideas were set out in his groundbreaking book "The Upright Ape: A new origin of species." More recently his article on "Homeotic Evolution in the Mammalia" has further expanded his thesis and enhanced his reputation.

In "The Upright Ape" he made it fairly clear that he regarded the homeotic transformation in the lumbar vertebra of Morotopithecus as purely random and instantaneous. Environmental influences had no bearing on it. Indeed he seems to feel
that an excessive interest in the life-style of the ancestral phenotype is a preoccupation of people he describes as "Darwin's acolytes". In the 288 pages of "The Upright Ape", reference to Moroto's surroundings is limited to six words: it lived "in the forest, at water's edge."

While I was happy about the last three words, I continue to be an unashamed acolyte of Charles Darwin. I have been surprised that no-one else seems to have demurred at the way his views are being progressively deleted from the official story of the evolution of life on earth. In The Upright Ape, there was one last concession to Darwinist thinking: the claim at one point that the random mutation might have been adaptive.

However, in the paper on "Homeotic Evolution" there are no indications of any lingering belief in Darwinism, and no references to competitive advantages, or natural selection. The paper is clearly designated as "A mutational view to update classic Darwinian and New Synthesis models of the past two centuries." "Update" appears to be a euphemism for "replace." I would like to cite a few reasons why I feel such deletion would be a mistake.

To return to Moroto: It is not easy to see how that mutated ancestral primate was able instantly to out-compete and outbreed all its contemporaries. The transverse process would have made it harder to walk on four legs, but by no means easier to walk on two. Bipedalism, even today, takes time for a newborn to acquire: the animal would have been born handicapped, and immobile for its first few months. Moving on two legs is more unstable: when trying to run on its unadapted hind limbs it would be far more liable to trip and fall, and for a biped damage to only one leg would have been fatally crippling. Furthermore, Moroto might have been female, and even if it were not, 50% of its descendants would have been. For them, bipedalism would render pregnancy and childbirth more painful and more dangerous, and child-rearing very much more arduous. It would be surprising if that mutation did not sputter out with the life of that individual, or within a century at the outside – unless the animals had lived in an environment where bipedalism might confer some significant advantage.

What environment? Why an advantage? Filler's suggestion in the book was that if the vertebral mutation had occurred in a monkey rather than an ape, it would have been a birth defect, and its possessor would not have survived to pass the mutation on to its descendants. However, if the mutation occurred in a more "upright" species, accustomed to suspensory postures such as arm-swinging, the new transverse process "would not have been a handicap." That is not a synonym for "would have been an advantage", but nevertheless, Darwin is now called in for the last time as an ally. As an ex-arm-swinger, Moroto would have had "the sine qua non of natural selection".

Would it? It all depends what you mean by "an upright species." The term urgently needs clarifying: it is also a point of contention between supporters of the water theory. It promotes the idea that hanging from a branch is a pre-adaptation for walking upright on the ground, since the animal is already accustomed to moving with its spine in a vertical plane. That seems highly unlikely. In branch-hangers, the lumbar vertebrae are maximally pulled apart by the weight of the legs and feet. That situation is at the furthest possible remove from the case of a biped, where these bones have to be entirely remodelled and enlarged and compressed for the new purpose of bearing the weight of the upper body. The vertical nature of branch-hangers is identical with the vertical nature of sheets hanging on a line, and nobody has ever described that as being "upright."

It still seems to me that the most obvious circumstance in which walking upright confers an advantage would be when wading through water. That is not mere fanciful speculation. It is not speculation at all:

it is observation. It refers to the only environment in which apes and monkeys do, still, regularly resort to walking on two legs. What reason is there to doubt that their ancestors did the same?

My main concern however is that the remarkable achievements of the evo/devo approach to science may be beginning to undermine the hard-won synthesis between the Mendelian and the Darwinian approaches. Two questions arise when any organism evolves. One is Darwin's question: "In what way did these changes improve the chances of the survival of the species?" The other is: "What alterations in their genetic make-up implemented those changes?" Recently there is a tendency in some quarters to regard the first of them as yesterday's question, no longer requiring an answer – and not getting one.

The two questions are indissolubly linked. Each dictates the parameters within which the other is free to operate. The power of an organism to adapt to environmental change is strictly limited by its genetic inheritance. Equally, the power of the chromosome to change over time is strictly limited by the ability of the individual phenotype to survive and procreate in the environment it inhabits.

Which is the more important?

That question is as pointless as looking at a drop of water and asking whether it is the oxygen or the hydrogen that makes it wet.